PLATO'S APO.
& PHAEDO

MW00978585

NOTES

including
- *Introduction*
- *Life of Socrates and Life of Plato*
- *Socrates' Discussion of Piety*
- *Socrates' Own Defense at His Trial*
- *Dialogs with Socrates during His Last Days and Hours*
- *Summaries and Commentaries*
- *Review Questions and Essay Topics*
- *Selected Bibliography*

by
Charles H. Patterson, Ph.D.
Professor of Philosophy, Emeritus
University of Nebraska

INCORPORATED

LINCOLN, NEBRASKA 68501

Editor

Gary Carey, M.A.
University of Colorado

Consulting Editor

James L. Roberts, Ph.D.
Department of English
University of Nebraska

ISBN 0-8220-1044-5
© Copyright 1975
by
Cliffs Notes, Inc.
All Rights Reserved
Printed in U.S.A.

1995 Printing

Cliffs Notes, Inc.   Lincoln, Nebraska

CONTENTS

Plato's Selected Dialogs of Socrates Notes

INTRODUCTION

The philosophy of ancient Greece reached its highest level of achievement in the works of Socrates, Plato, and Aristotle. The influence of these men on the culture of the Western world can scarcely be overestimated. Each of them made significant contributions to philosophy and it would be difficult to determine to which one of them we are most indebted. All three were original thinkers as well as great teachers. In point of time Socrates was the one who appeared first. Plato became the most distinguished of his pupils and Aristotle in turn received instruction from Plato. Both Plato and Aristotle were prolific writers and what we know about them has been derived chiefly from their published works. In contrast to them, Socrates left no writings at all. Consequently, what information we have concerning him comes from the testimony of others who were associated with him and who were influenced both by the moral quality of his living and the significance of the ideas that he expounded.

On the basis of what has been reported concerning Socrates, we would judge that he made a profound impression upon a group of his followers who were closely associated with his life and teachings. The name of Socrates has been revered throughout the centuries and he has been regarded as one of the greatest teachers of all time. Plato, in one of his best known dialogs, refers to Socrates as a friend "whom I may truly call the wisest, and justest, and best of all men whom I have ever known." Although Socrates was never deified by the Greeks in the sense in which Jesus has been deified by Christians, it is interesting to note some of the striking similarities that have characterized both of their lives. For instance, both men were teachers of great distinction. Neither of them left any writings of his own. Both conducted their teaching activities by means of conversations with individuals. Both men were critical of the religious and political leaders of their time. Each of them proclaimed by precept and example a standard of moral conduct above that which prevailed among the recognized leaders of the society in which he lived. Both of them suffered a martyr's death. Finally, there is a sense in which each of them arose from the dead by virtue of the fact that his teachings and the causes that he served became more alive and powerful after his death than during the times when he was living.

Plato and Aristotle have been held in high esteem because of their intellectual achievements and the fact that their ideas have been preserved through the writings that they produced. Socrates has also been recognized as an intellectual genius, but in addition, his career in the city of Athens has come to be regarded by many persons as an outstanding example of the virtues that he advocated. His humility, intellectual honesty, devotion to the public good, and loyalty to what he believed was morally right exemplify his conception of what constitutes the good life. Because of the quality of his living, along with the abiding truth of what he taught, the story of his trial and death is something that will continue to stir the imagination of people and to win for him their admiration and respect.

LIFE OF SOCRATES

Although Socrates left no written records concerning himself, it is possible to reconstruct a fairly accurate account of his life from the writings of his Greek contemporaries. Aristophanes caricatured him in a work called *The Clouds*. Xenophon in his *Memorabilia* expressed high praise for Socrates, with special reference to the method that he advocated for selecting the rulers of a state. Plato, to whom we are most indebted for information about Socrates, made him the chief character in many of his famous dialogs. It is generally assumed that in Plato's earlier dialogs the speeches attributed to Socrates are historical in the sense that they reproduce what Socrates actually said in the conversations he held with fellow Athenians. In the later dialogs there is reason to believe that, at least in some instances, Plato was setting forth his own ideas by putting them into the mouth of Socrates. To what extent this was done is something that cannot be known with certainty.

Socrates was born in the city of Athens in 469 B.C. He was the son of poor parents, his father being a sculptor and his mother a midwife. Early in life he took up the occupation of his father and continued in it for a relatively brief period of time. Later he volunteered for service as a soldier in the Peloponnesian War. In the campaigns in which he fought, he showed himself to be a brave and loyal member of the fighting force. After his retirement from the army, the most of his adult life was spent in response to what he believed to be a divine command to devote his time and energies to the pursuit of wisdom. It was in this connection that he felt called upon to examine himself by questioning other men. Accordingly, it was his custom to engage in conversation with all sorts and conditions of men and women on the streets, in the marketplace, or wherever it was convenient for them to meet. Their discussions covered a wide range of subjects, including such topics as love, marriage, politics, war, friendship, poetry, religion, science, government, and morals. The method that Socrates used in these discussions is known as *dialectic*. It consisted of conversations, the purpose of which was to bring to light the implications involved in different points of view and thus to expose the errors that they contained. He had a keen mind and was quick to discover the fallacies in an argument and he was skillful in steering the conversations toward the very heart of the matter.

With regard to his personal appearance, it is said that Socrates was most unattractive. It is reported that he was short, stout, snub-nosed, and careless about his dress. However, these peculiarities were quickly forgotten by those who listened to his conversations. As soon as he began to speak, his listeners were charmed by his wit, his good humor, and his kindly disposition. His brilliant discourses, which covered a wide range of subjects, brought admiration and respect on the part of those who participated in the conversations with him. He was especially concerned with the subject of moral conduct. He not only talked about the virtues that are an essential part of the good life, but he exemplified in his own living the virtues that he taught others should seek for themselves. For example, he possessed to a remarkable degree the virtue of self-control. He never boasted of his own achievements. He was humble and intellectually honest. He was magnanimous in his attitude toward others. He was noble in character, frugal in his living, and a person of great endurance.

He is remembered not only for the quality of his living but for the content of his teachings. He believed that the most important topic that can occupy the mind of man is the meaning of the good life. He had no quarrel with the physicists and natural scientists of his day, who were trying to obtain a descriptive account of the way things are and the laws that govern their behavior. Important as this type of information might be, it was a matter of far greater significance to understand the meaning of human life and the way that men ought to live. The physical sciences do not reveal anything concerning the purpose for which things exist nor do they tell us anything about the nature of goodness. They do not reveal what is good or bad nor do they distinguish between what is morally right and wrong. A far more important type of inquiry has to do with knowledge of what constitutes the good life.

Although he rejected the popular conceptions of the Greek gods and their relation to human beings, Socrates believed that a divine providence had to do with the creation of the world and, further, that the purpose toward which it was directed was the achievement of the good life on the part of human beings. Man was something more than a physical organism. His body was the dwelling place of the soul and what happens to the soul was vastly more important than what happens to the body.

An epitome of Socrates' moral philosophy can be expressed briefly in the statement "virtue is knowledge." Virtues, he taught, are acquired through a fulfillment of the purpose for which one exists. In the case of a man, this would mean the harmonious development of the elements found in human nature and this would apply to life as a whole rather than just the present moment or the immediate future. The knowledge to which this statement refers is something more than an awareness of facts concerning the order of the material universe. It involves an understanding of the soul in relation to the good life. It was Socrates' conviction that ignorance concerning the good life was the chief cause of the evil that men do. He did not believe that anyone would knowingly do that which was harmful to himself. Virtue alone is capable of bringing satisfaction to the soul. Although this is the goal toward which everyone strives, not everyone reaches it. Their failures are due to the fact that they do not know what will bring lasting satisfaction. They pursue sensuous pleasures, material wealth, public esteem, and similar goals, thinking that these will bring about the greatest amount of happiness. When any one or all of these goals has been reached, they discover that objectives of this type do not bring about peace of mind nor do they meet the demands of one's true or real self. It is only through the proper development of the mind in its pursuit of truth, beauty, and goodness that the goal and purpose of human life can be achieved.

Because knowledge concerning the meaning of the good life was an essential requirement for making proper decisions with regard to the welfare of the community, Socrates was especially critical of a democratic form of government in which a given society is ruled by the majority of its citizens, regardless of their qualifications for understanding the issues upon which they must make decisions. He pointed out that in any other line of activity only those persons with the necessary qualifications would be selected for the job. For example, if one wanted to have his shoes repaired he would employ a shoemaker. If he wanted to build a house he would hire a carpenter, or if he wanted someone to manage a particular line of business he would select someone who by his training and experience would have demonstrated that he had the ability to perform successfully. Those who are called upon to govern the state are asked to make decisions that are far more important than those having to do with the lesser affairs of everyday living. For this reason they ought to possess both intellectual and moral qualifications that are above the average. Athenian democracy in the age of Socrates did not insist on a high standard of qualifications for those who would rule the state. Hence, it followed that in many instances persons would be elected to high office and entrusted with extraordinary power, even though they lacked both the will and the ability to govern the state in accordance with the best interests of the people.

When Socrates would call attention to these shortcomings on the part of elected officials who were unprepared for their duties, he incurred the wrath of those whom he had criticized. As a general rule, people do not like to have their defects pointed out to them, and when this does occur they usually show their resentment by launching an attack on the person who has questioned their qualifications. Whether their accusations are based on facts appears to make no difference, since their purpose is to arouse sentiment against the individual who has charged them with incompetency. This is what happened when Socrates pointed out that Meletus, a member of the governing Council, was ill-prepared for the decisions he was called upon to make. Meletus, along with Anytus, Lycon, and others who belonged to the same group, retaliated by charging that Socrates had rejected the gods of Athens, was a corrupter of the youth, and an enemy of the state. Meletus even insisted that Socrates was an atheist and that his teachings would bring about an utter collapse of public morality.

In reply to these charges Socrates made a noble defense of his manner of living. He presented sufficient evidence to show that the accusations brought against him were without adequate foundation. Nevertheless, when the issue was put to a vote a majority of the judges voted against him and thus Socrates was sentenced to die. When given the opportunity to propose an alternate sentence, he asked that the state provide for him in a manner that would be appropriate for one of its chief benefactors. This alternative was rejected and Socrates was placed in jail to await his execution. Although he had ample opportunity to escape and several of his friends urged him to do so, Socrates refused to follow their advice, stating that it was his duty to see to it that the laws of the state were obeyed. His execution was delayed for a period of thirty days because of an Athenian tradition that maintained that the period of time taken by the passage of a ship to and from the island of Delos was regarded as holy and no execution of a criminal could take place during that interval. While waiting for the ship to return, Socrates was visited by a number of his friends, who came not only for the purpose of expressing their sympathy but for another opportunity of carrying on conversations with the master whom they had come to love and admire. The jailer who had charge of the prison treated Socrates very kindly and would have allowed him to escape if he would have been willing to do so. Socrates had no fear of death, which could only do harm to the body but was powerless to injure the soul. He regarded loyalty to what he believed was right as more important than mere physical survival. After bidding good-bye to the members of his family and having a final discourse with friends who had come to be with him during his last hours, he cheerfully submitted to the penalty that had been imposed upon him and drank the poison that the jailer handed to him.

LIFE OF PLATO

Among those who were influenced by the life and teachings of Socrates no one has done more to perpetuate his memory than Plato, who has long been recognized as one of the greatest philosophers of ancient Greece and one of the most profound thinkers of all time. Plato was too young to have been one of Socrates' most intimate friends. It was not until the last seven or eight years of Socrates' life that Plato came under his influence, but those years made a lasting impression on his life and determined to a large extent the future course of his life. In his later years Plato is reported to have said

"I thank God that I was born Greek and not barbarian, free and not slave, male and not female, but above all that I was born in the age of Socrates."

Owing to the fact that he was ill at the time, Plato was not present when a group of Socrates' friends came to the prison for their last visit with him. However, he had been so deeply impressed by the moral quality of Socrates' teachings and his devotion to the cause of truth and justice that he determined to perpetuate his memory by writing a series of biographical dialogs in which his true character would be brought to light. Even after Plato's own thought had matured he continued to make Socrates the protagonist of his dialogs. The result has been such a blending of views that in several instances it is difficult, if not impossible, to tell where the actual historical Socrates leaves off and Plato's own thought begins.

Plato was born in the city of Athens in the year 427 B.C. He died in the year 347 B.C. He came from an aristocratic family that for a long time had been identified with leadership in Athens. His father, Ariston, was a descendant of King Codrus and his mother, whose name was Perictione, claimed to have been descended from the famous lawgiver Solon. As a boy he was named Aristocles, but because of his broad shoulders and forehead, he was called Plato and it is by this name that he has become known to posterity. During his youth he gained distinction as an athlete and was also recognized for his extraordinary mental abilities. In addition to his achievements along these lines, his social standing and connections would have made him an outstanding individual in any career he might have entered.

He lived during a critical period of Greek history. His youth saw the decline and fall of Athenian power but not of Athenian genius. His early education began under the supervision of private tutors who were well known for their professional skills. Under their guidance he received instruction in the elementary disciplines, such as gymnastics, music, reading, writing, and the study of numbers. After reaching the age of eighteen or thereabouts, he spent two years in military training, which placed considerable emphasis on physical exercises and the proper care of the body. This was followed by a more advanced period of study in which he gained familiarity with several of the more prominent schools of Greek philosophy. This gave to him an opportunity to become acquainted with many of the Sophists, who were the recognized professional teachers of that time. Finally, Plato spent about seven or eight years as a pupil of Socrates. This experience influenced him, not only to devote the rest of his life to philosophy, but to carry on his career in the spirit and under the guidance of his beloved teacher.

Because Socrates had been put to death under the auspices of the Athenian government, Plato believed that it would not be safe for him to remain in the city and thus expose himself to the same kind of treatment. It was well known that Plato had been one of Socrates' followers and that he was most sympathetic toward the ideas that his teacher had proclaimed. So long as these ideas were regarded as harmful to the state, anyone who subscribed to them would be in danger. For this reason Plato left the city of Athens for a time and journeyed to a number of different places, where he hoped to become better acquainted with the leaders of a number of philosophical movements. At first he went to Megara, where he carried on conversations with Euclid, the famous mathematician. Later, he made extensive journeys to Egypt, Cyrene, Crete, and southern Italy. These excursions gave him an opportunity to become better acquainted with the leaders of each of the schools founded, respectively, by Pythagoras, Heraclitus, and the Eleatic philosophers.

When Plato was approximately forty years of age, he undertook an experiment in government. From his early youth he had been interested in political affairs. From his associations with Socrates and from his own observations, he had arrived at certain convictions concerning the proper qualifications for those whose duty it was to govern the state. He believed that only those persons who possessed intellectual as well as moral qualities should be entrusted with the power to rule over others. Eventually, the opportunity came to him to put his philosophy into practice. At Syracuse, on the coast of the island of Sicily, a friend and pupil by the name of Dion urged him to undertake the education of Dionysius, the tyrant of Syracuse. Dionysius appeared to be willing to take instruction from Plato, and this would make it possible for Plato's theory of government to be tried out under actual conditions. The experiment was not a success, for Dionysius was not an apt pupil, and when Plato rebuked him for his stupidity, the tyrant retaliated by having Plato put in chains and sentenced to death. Dion used his influence to get the sentence changed. The result was that Plato's life was spared but at the price of being made a slave. Soon afterward Anniceris, a member of the Cyrenaic school of philosophy, came to Syracuse and purchased Plato's freedom, thus allowing him to return to Athens.

After returning to Athens, Plato established his school, an institution that came to be known as the *Academy*. It continued for a period of more than eight centuries as a center for the study and evaluation of Platonic philosophy. With the establishment of the Academy, Plato devoted the most of his time to teaching and the writing of dialogs. Fortunately, the most of these dialogs have been preserved and they constitute the chief source of the information we have concerning the various aspects of his philosophy.

According to the accounts given of Plato's life, on two more occasions his career as a teacher and writer was interrupted by further attempts to reconstruct the government of Syracuse. After the death of Dionysius, he was urged again by Dion to undertake the education of the younger Dionysius, who now ruled in the place formerly held by his father. Again the experiment failed to achieve the desired results. Reluctantly, Plato decided to give it up and he returned to Athens convinced that the education of people in powerful positions cannot be accomplished without their cooperation. We are told that he later made a third and final attempt to apply his political philosophy at Syracuse but with results similar to the ones he had experienced before. This time he was saved from the wrath of Dionysius by the good offices of his friend Archytas of Tarentum. Returning to Athens, he devoted the rest of his life to teaching and writing. He died in 347 B.C. According to one account his death occurred peacefully while he was attending a wedding feast at the home of a friend.

Plato used the dialog form of writing as the most effective means of presenting his philosophical views. There were several reasons for doing this. In the first place, it was not his intention to answer specific questions or to propose final and dogmatic solutions to any of the problems that were being discussed. He preferred instead to do something that would stimulate original thinking on the part of the reader. Second, this manner of presentation enabled him to present contrasting points of view as they would be likely to occur in a series of conversations taking place among individuals having different points of view. This would help to prepare the way for any reader of the dialogs to arrive at his own conclusion, after giving some consideration to each of the views that had been presented. Finally, by using the conversational method it would be possible to illustrate the way in which current issues of the day were related to one another. This is one of the reasons why no one of Plato's dialogs is devoted exclusively to the discussion of a single topic. He wanted to make it clear that in order to understand any particular subject you must see how it is related to other subjects and to the field of knowledge as a whole.

As a general rule, Plato did not mention his own name as the author of a particular point of view. However, in many of the dialogs we are fairly safe in assuming that what Plato himself believed about the topic under discussion is contained in the speeches attributed to Socrates. Several of the other characters used in the dialogs were well-known Sophists. The statements attributed to them constitute one of the main sources for our information about the Sophistic movement in ancient Greece.

Plato wrote more than thirty dialogs, all of which have been preserved, either in their original form or as they have been edited and translated by competent scholars who have specialized in the area of Greek philosophy. There is no way of knowing the exact order in which the dialogs were written nor is there any complete agreement on this point among historians of philosophy. It is, however, generally assumed that the earlier ones have to do primarily with the field of ethics. In these dialogs Socrates is presented as an inquirer concerning the precise meaning of specific virtues. The Sophists with whom he is holding conversation profess to have a complete understanding of the virtues in question and they do not hesitate to make statements concerning their meanings and contents. Socrates claims that he is ignorant of these matters but he begins to question the Sophists about the statements they have made. The purpose of this questioning is to bring to light some of the implications involved in what they have said and thus to show the inadequacies of their professed wisdom. This is usually done by revealing the self-contradictory character of their statements or in what respects they are not in harmony with known facts. Without presenting any final answer to the questions that have been raised, Socrates advises his listeners to continue the search for a better understanding of the virtues and their relation to the good life.

Plato's philosophy as a whole covers a wide range of subjects, which are treated at considerable length in various parts of different dialogs. No one of the dialogs is devoted exclusively to the treatment of a single topic, for the questions that arise in connection with any one of them are necessarily related to different areas of experience and Plato wanted the discussions in the dialogs to correspond as nearly as possible to the situations that occur in human life. Nevertheless, it is possible in certain instances to indicate the theme that is the predominant one in a particular dialog. For example, Plato's theory of knowledge is the chief subject matter found in the *Meno* and again in the *Theaetetus*. His theory of Ideas, which is implicit in all of the dialogs, is subjected to a critical examination in the *Parmenides*. His cosmology, along with a theory of creation, is given special treatment in the *Timaeus*. His philosophy concerning the place of pleasure in the good life is set forth in the *Philebus*. The best known and the most widely used of Plato's dialogs is *The Republic*. Its chief purpose was to set forth the author's theory of government, but in relation to this topic there are discussions of nearly all of the more important aspects of his philosophical position. *The Republic* has often been considered to be the greatest of the dialogs, although there are many commentators who would not agree. It represents what Plato regarded as the ideal toward which actual states should strive. In a later and considerably longer dialog called *The Laws*, he proposed a less idealistic but more practical alternative for the organization of state governments.

With reference to the trial and death of Socrates there are four dialogs that are especially relevant. They are the *Euthyphro*, the *Apology*, the *Crito*, and the *Phaedo*. In the *Euthyphro* an attempt is made to answer the question "What is piety?" It has a particular bearing on the trial of Socrates, for he had been accused of impiety and was about to be tried for a crime, the nature of which no one seemed to understand. The *Apology* contains an account of Socrates' defense of himself after he had been charged with being a corrupter of the youth and one who refuses to accept the popular beliefs concerning the gods of the city of Athens. It is generally regarded as the most authentic account on record of what Socrates actually said as he appeared before his judges. The *Crito* is an account of the conversation that takes place in the jail where Socrates is confined awaiting his execution. He is visited by Crito, an aged and trusted friend, who has come to the prison for the purpose of trying to persuade Socrates to avoid being put to death either by an escape from the prison where he is being held or by employing some other means. The dialog depicts Socrates as a man who has no fear of death and one who would rather die than commit an act that he believes to be morally wrong. The *Phaedo* is a narrative concerning the last hours in the life of Socrates. After an interval of years, the story is related to Echecrates by Phaedo, who was one of Socrates' beloved disciples. The narration takes place at Phlius, which is the home of Phaedo. The scene of the story is the prison where Socrates is held. Phaedo is one of a number of friends who have gathered for their last meeting with Socrates. Much of the discussion that takes place has to do with Socrates' attitude toward death, including his reasons for believing in the immortality of the soul.

Plato's dialogs have been translated into many different languages and they have been published in a number of editions. One of the best known translations in English is the one made by Benjamin Jowett of Oxford University in England. It was first published during the latter half of the nineteenth century. Since that time other translations have been made that are regarded as improvements in some respects over the one made by Jowett. So far as our study of the last days of Socrates is concerned the changes that have been made in the more recent translations are of minor importance and for this reason our study of the four dialogs that are included in these notes will be based on the Jowett translation. The quotations that are used both in the summaries of the dialogs and the commentaries that follow are taken from this translation.

SUMMARIES AND COMMENTARIES

EUTHYPHRO

Summary

Plato's dialog called *Euthyphro* relates a discussion that took place between Socrates and Euthyphro concerning the meaning of piety, or that virtue usually regarded as a manner of living that fulfills one's duty both to gods and to men. It is of particular interest in relation to the fate of Socrates, inasmuch as he has recently been charged with impiety and is about to be tried before the Athenian court to determine his guilt or innocence of the crime attributed to him. Because he felt quite sure that the Athenian people in general did not understand the real nature of either piety or impiety,

Socrates asks Euthyphro to answer the question "What is piety?" He has a real purpose in doing this, for Euthyphro, a Sophist, professes to be wise concerning such matters, while Socrates, making no such claim for himself, professes only to be ignorant. He wants to see if Euthyphro is as wise as he claims to be, and if he is not, Socrates will expose the shallowness of his claim.

Euthyphro has the reputation of being a wise person, a diviner, and a soothsayer. As a teacher he gives instruction on moral and political matters, as well as the practical problems of everyday living. The discussion that is carried on between Socrates and Euthyphro takes place on the porch of King Archon. Both Socrates and Euthyphro are involved in matters of a legal nature. Socrates has been accused of impiety and is facing a court trial. Euthyphro is the plaintiff in a forthcoming trial for murder. Socrates asks who it is who is being charged with this crime. He is surprised and shocked to learn that Euthyphro is bringing this charge against his own father. The circumstances bringing this about have a direct bearing on the case. It appears that a poor dependent of the Euthyphro family had killed one of their domestic servants. At the command of Euthyphro's father the guilty person had been bound and thrown into a ditch. Messengers had then been sent to Athens to inquire of the interpreters of religion concerning what should be done with him. By the time these messengers had returned the criminal had died from hunger and exposure. Euthyphro's father was, at least to some extent, responsible for the offender's death and this was the basis for charging him with the crime of murder.

Socrates is impressed by the fact that Euthyphro is willing to perform his duty in the matter, even though it means taking action against a member of his own family. Without any further discussion of the case involving Euthyphro's father, Socrates is anxious to pursue inquiry concerning the nature of piety, since this is directly related to the fact that Meletus has accused him of the crime of impiety. Accordingly, he addresses this question to Euthyphro, "What is piety?" Euthyphro answers at once that piety is acting the way he is acting in bringing charges against one who has done wrong, even though that person happens to be his own father. Although admitting that Euthyphro is right in not allowing personal relationships to stand in the way of performing his duty, Socrates is not satisfied with the answer that has been given to his question. An example of the virtue of piety is not equivalent to a definition of that virtue. Euthyphro has given but one example, and even though he defended his statement by mentioning that certain of the Greek gods have acted in a similar manner, Socrates insists that a proper definition of piety must be sufficient to include all instances of that virtue. Euthyphro's statement has not been adequate for this purpose. Nevertheless, Socrates insists that, inasmuch as Euthyphro has brought a criminal charge against his own father, he must have known the nature of impiety or he would have been unable to decide that his father was guilty of it. Once again he urges Euthyphro to tell him what piety is. If he can obtain a satisfactory answer to this question, it will enable him to know whether the charge that Meletus is bringing against him is a well-founded one.

In reply Euthyphro advances another statement. He says "Piety is what is dear to the gods and impiety is that which is not dear to them." Upon examination by Socrates, this statement turns out to be no more satisfactory than the former one. It is not clear what makes anything dear to the gods, and besides, there is the question of whether that which is dear to some of the gods is dear to all of them or only to some of them. Euthyphro then insists that piety is that which is pleasing to all of the gods. He feels sure they all agree that murder is wrong. Socrates then points out that the circumstances under which killing takes place makes an important difference concerning the moral quality of the act. The same is true with reference to the motive that was involved. It is quite evident that so far the discussion has not produced any satisfactory answer to the question concerning the nature of piety.

To approach the subject in a different way, Socrates asks Euthyphro if people who are pious are also just? Yes, says Euthyphro, but at the same time he recognizes that it is not true that all just persons are pious. Socrates then wants to know if piety is a part of justice and if it is of what part does it consist? Euthyphro replies that piety is that part of justice that attends to the gods, just as there is another part of justice that attends to men. This, too, is unsatisfactory because we do not know what "attends" means. When applied to some things such as dogs, horses, and men, it implies some way of making them better. When applied to gods it cannot have this meaning, since there is no respect in which men can make the gods better than they are. At this point Euthyphro states that there are various ways in which men can minister to the gods, but he does not have the time to point them out.

Socrates still insists that he does not know what piety is and certainly Euthyphro has not revealed its true nature. The question is an important one, not only for Socrates, but for anyone who is called upon to make decisions relative to moral conduct. The dialog closes without any final answer to the question with which the discussion started. Socrates urges Euthyphro to continue the search for the meaning of piety. Until he has found it there can be no justification for the decision he has made concerning his father.

Commentary

For those who are looking for a satisfactory definition of piety, the dialog is a disappointment, for no conclusion has been reached concerning the precise nature of that virtue. It has sometimes been maintained that the true purpose of philosophy is not to answer questions but rather to question the answers that have been given. At any rate, this is exactly what Socrates has been doing in this dialog. Euthyphro has presented several quick and ready answers to the question "What is piety?" but upon examination each of them has been shown to be unsatisfactory. The method which Socrates has used is known as *dialectic*. It consists of pointing out the inconsistencies and self-contradictions involved in popular statements made without thinking about their logical implications. In this instance, the use of this method has not only brought to light the shallowness of popular conceptions held by many of the Sophists but it serves as a defense of Socrates by revealing something of the character of the man and the type of work in which he has been engaged.

Socrates has been accused of teaching false doctrines and thereby corrupting the youth of Athens. This is the kind of charge that has frequently been made concerning philosophers and it is for this reason that action has often been taken against them. While it is admitted that everyone is entitled to think as he pleases, the trouble arises when one tries to persuade other people to think as he does. That Socrates is not guilty of the charges brought against him can be seen from the fact that he has not been trying to indoctrinate anyone. He does not claim that his own views are perfect or that he has arrived at the final truth concerning the matter under consideration. Instead, his role is that of the inquirer and his purpose is to get people to think for themselves. In fact, one of his chief criticisms of the Sophists is that they accept too readily what has been told to them by others, without ever stopping to consider the evidence upon which it has been based.

It is true that getting people to think for themselves does have its dangers and this to some extent accounts for the opposition that has been raised against Socrates. Clear and correct thinking is bound to expose the errors upon which popular conceptions are often based. It also tends to bring to light the defects of those who pretend to know far more than is actually the case or who boast of qualifications that they do not possess. Those whose defects have thus been pointed out naturally have a feeling of resentment toward the person who has been responsible for bringing it about. This is one of the reasons why Meletus has been bringing charges against Socrates. It is easier to find fault with the person who is your critic than it is to admit the truth of what he has been saying.

Although Euthyphro as a Sophist exhibits some of the conceit and arrogance that is characteristic of that group as a whole, he is not to be regarded as a man who is altogether bad. He does have some redeeming qualities. He is a conscientious person and in this respect he is ready to perform what he believes to be his duty to the gods, even though it involves bringing charges against his own father. It appears that what Euthyphro's father has done under the existing circumstances was justifiable under Athenian law and it was quite unlikely that he would be punished. Nevertheless, Euthyphro believes it is his religious duty to report what his father has done and that is his main reason for doing it. Having fulfilled his duty in regard to the event, his conscience will be at peace. Furthermore, Euthyphro is very much opposed to Meletus and on many points he is in complete agreement with Socrates.

In harmony with many of his fellow Athenians, Euthyphro conceives of piety in terms of religion and this involves a relationship between gods and men. This relationship is understood to mean a process of giving and receiving. Prayers and sacrifices are given to the gods, who in return bestow material benefits on their worshipers. This is obviously what Euthyphro had in mind when he stated that piety is doing that which is dear to the gods and impiety is doing that which is not pleasing to the gods. When asked what it is that makes something dear to the gods, the reply is that it is attending to their wishes and this is accomplished by making sacrifices to them and by offering prayers of praise and thanksgiving.

One of the purposes of this dialog is to contrast two very different conceptions of religion. One of these is illustrated in Euthyphro's view of religion as a kind of mercenary process. It was a fairly popular view in the city of Athens, just as it has been held by many persons in other times and places. Making gifts to the gods and receiving benefits from them implied in Euthyphro's case a belief in the reality of the Athenian gods as set forth in popular stories concerning their behavior and their supernatural power. The other conception of religion is the one held by Socrates. He did not accept as literally true many of the popular tales concerning the activities of the gods. It was for this reason that Meletus and others had accused him of being irreligious and undermining the faith of the youth. The accusation was not a just one, for the fact that Socrates did not accept the conception of the gods held by other persons did not imply that he held no belief in divinity at all. As a matter of fact, Socrates was in one sense of the word a very devout and religious person. Evidence of this can be seen in his attitude with reference to the mystical voice that warned him not to do certain things. This voice, to which he often referred, was regarded as a divine voice and he always paid heed to it. Further than this, Socrates held that a divine purpose was expressed in the creation of the world and this purpose was directed toward the moral and spiritual development of human beings.

In the discussion that takes place about piety in relation to justice, Socrates rejects Euthyphro's distinction between service to the gods and service to men. He does so for several reasons. In the first place, he does not believe that one's duty toward a divine being should be regarded as something that is separate and distinct from his duty toward his fellow men. On the contrary, he holds that the only true way of rendering service to God consists in doing what one can to promote the moral and spiritual development of human beings. Second, Socrates regards the purpose and function of religion as something that is quite different from the view expressed by Euthyphro. Instead of religion being used as a kind of tool or device for getting what one wants, as was true in Euthyphro's case, Socrates believes the primary purpose of true religion is to bring one's own life into harmony with the will of God. Religion and morality, in his view, are so closely related that neither one can exist apart from the other. Unlike the Sophists, who were accustomed to think of the demands of morality as nothing more than the desires of the people who formulated them, Socrates believes in a standard of morality that is something more than human opinion. He identifies it with the will of God.

APOLOGY

Summary

The *Apology* is believed to be the most authentic account that has been preserved of Socrates' defense of himself as it was presented before the Athenian Council. It is in essential harmony with the references to the trial that occur in Plato's other dialogs and also with the account given in Xenophon's *Memorabilia*. It appears to record, in many instances, the exact words used by Socrates while making his speech in defense of himself. To be sure, the words were not recorded at the time they were spoken but we know that Plato was present at the trial, and hence we may conclude that the account given in the *Apology* contains the words of Socrates as they were remembered by Plato. However, we should bear in mind that Plato had been both a pupil and an ardent admirer of Socrates and for this reason his version of the trial may have been somewhat biased in favor of the one whom he regarded as a truly great hero. At any rate, we may be fairly certain that, even though Socrates has been to some extent idealized by his pupil, the account given represents what Plato believed to be true about his teacher. It is also possible that Socrates' defense of himself was even stronger than what has been reported.

The contents of the dialog include a number of different parts. The first one consists of an introductory statement that Socrates makes concerning the manner of his speaking. This is followed by an account of the specific accusations made with reference to his life and daily activities. Socrates replies at some length to each of the charges brought against him. After making his defense, an account is given of his attempt at mitigation of the penalty imposed on him. Finally, Socrates makes a prophetic rebuke of the judges for supposing they will live at ease and with an untroubled conscience after pronouncing sentence as a penalty for his crimes.

The dialog begins with Socrates making a short speech in which he offers an apology for the colloquial style in which he will be making his defense. His accusers have warned the judges to be on their guard lest they be deceived by the eloquence of Socrates in his attempt to convince them of his innocence. Socrates insists that he makes no claim of being eloquent in his speech. He is not a rhetorician and they should be ashamed for suggesting that he would try to lead them astray by the force of his eloquence. The only kind of eloquence for which he has any use is that which sets forth the truth in language so plain that they can all understand. That is a very different kind of eloquence from the one they have implied in their warning to the judges. Socrates tells them that he will indeed speak the truth and he implores the judges not to be thinking of the manner of his speech but only of the justice of the cause for which he pleads.

In making his defense Socrates will reply to two kinds of accusations. The first one is referred to as the older or more ancient accusation and the second one is the contemporary charge being made by Meletus, Anytus, and others who are present at the trial. It is the first, or older, accusation that he dreads most of all. The reason for this is that his accusers are many and he cannot call them all by name. Most of them are not present and thus he is unable to give them the opportunity to reply to what he has to say. The accusations go back over a period of many years and may be summed up in the following words. "Socrates is an evil-doer, and a curious person, who searches into things under the earth and in heaven, and he makes the worse appear the better cause; and he teaches the aforesaid doctrines to others."

Asserting that these accusations are based entirely on falsehoods, Socrates points out that they have given him a bad reputation over the years. As an example, he mentions the fact that Aristophanes in his comedy play called the *Clouds* has referred to a man called Socrates who goes about claiming that he can walk on air and pretending to a lot of other nonsense concerning matters of which there is no element of truth. While it is quite possible that Aristophanes did not intend these statements to be taken seriously, they have nevertheless contributed toward the unfavorable opinion that has been formed about him. Another factor that has been working against him is the rumor that has been circulated concerning his investigations of things in heaven above and in the earth beneath. These, too, are based on falsehoods, for he has had no interest in the physical sciences and he has never claimed to have any wisdom about matters of this kind. This does not mean that he has any quarrel with the physical scientists. He recognizes the legitimacy of what they are doing but he has preferred to give his attention to other matters, especially the ones that have to do with moral conduct and the welfare of the soul.

A further explanation of the way in which these rumors were started can be seen in the account of the wisdom that Socrates is said to claim for himself. The story came about in the following manner. A certain man called

Chaerephon had inquired of the oracle of Delphi whether there was anyone wiser than Socrates? The oracle had answered the question in the negative, thus making it clear that Socrates was indeed the wisest of all the men in Athens. When this was reported to Socrates he was amazed, for he had never considered himself to be a wise person. To determine whether the assertion made by the oracle was true he began a series of inquiries and investigations. He went to a number of different persons, each one of whom claimed to be wise and was so regarded by his fellow citizens. In each case the reputation of the individual was an ill-founded one, for upon being questioned and examined by Socrates it became evident that they did not possess the wisdom attributed to them. He went to one man who was a politician and who had the reputation of wisdom, but when Socrates began to talk with him it became clear that he was not as wise as he had supposed himself to be. When Socrates pointed this out to him, the result was that the politician began to hate him, and his enmity toward the one who had exposed his ignorance was shared by several of those who were present and overheard the conversation. Nevertheless, Socrates concludes that he is better off than the individual whom he has just examined, for that person knows nothing but thinks that he knows while Socrates neither knows nor thinks that he knows. The oracle at Delphi was correct in his statement. Socrates is wiser than any of the others because he is aware of his own ignorance and they are not.

After his encounter with the politician, Socrates went to one man after another, trying desperately to determine whether the statement made by the oracle was indeed the truth. He went to the poets, and after asking them to explain some of the most elaborate passages in their own writings, he found they had no understanding of the things they had written. They even insisted that their poetry was not the product of wisdom but of a kind of inspiration like that of the diviners and soothsayers. Leaving the poets, he went to the artisans but again he observed they fell into the same error as the poets, for while they did have knowledge of some things, they were ignorant concerning matters of the greatest importance. As a result of his investigations, he reports to the Athenians that he found the men most in repute were all but the most foolish and that some inferior men were really wiser and better than those held in high esteem. Although his mission had convinced him that the oracle had spoken the truth, it nevertheless had the unfortunate consequence of making for him a large number of enemies and this has given rise to a whole series of calumnies that have befallen him.

Again Socrates points out another source of the prejudice against him that has developed over the years. Some of the young men of the wealthier class have been attracted to him because they enjoy listening to the way in which he exposes the ignorance of those who claim to be wise. They observe that those who are examined and found to be wanting in wisdom instead of becoming angry with themselves become angry with Socrates and call him a villainous misleader of youth, a dangerous character, and one whose influence should be brought to an end. Their accusations arouse a great deal of curiosity on the part of people in general. When they inquire of the youth who have been listening to the discussions what the evil teaching is of which Socrates is accused, these young men are unable to tell. However, in order to appear that they are not at a loss to know what it is all about, they repeat the charges they have heard about philosophers teaching things up in the clouds and under the earth and making the worse appear to be the better cause. Because the people making these charges are numerous and energetic and have persuasive tongues, they have filled the ears of many with their loud and inveterate calumnies. This is the reason why Meletus, Anytus, and others have charged him with crimes and are bringing him to trial.

Having made his defense against the first class of his accusers, Socrates proceeds to reply to the specific charges that are now being made against him. Meletus has stated that Socrates is a doer of evil, in that he corrupts the youth, does not believe in the gods of the state, and has introduced new divinities of his own. To defend himself against these charges, Socrates asks Meletus to come forward and answer some questions. Socrates is especially skillful in the questions he asks of his adversary, with the result that Meletus is shown to be contradicting himself and making accusations that are utterly absurd. His statements imply that Socrates is the only one in the city of Athens who is corrupting the youth. Everyone else is working for their improvement. At the same time, he admits that no one would intentionally make the people worse so long as he is obliged to live among them. From this it follows either that Socrates is not making the people worse or he is doing so unintentionally. In either case he is guilty of no crime and ought not be punished. Obviously, Meletus does not understand the nature of the charges he is making nor is he able to see the logical consequences implied in the statements he has been making.

Socrates then asks Meletus to state how it is that he is corrupting the youth? Is it that he is teaching them not to acknowledge the gods that the state acknowledges but some other divinities or spiritual agencies in place of them? Or does he insist that Socrates is an atheist and does not believe in any god at all? Meletus replies that Socrates is an atheist, inasmuch as he does not believe in the godhead of the sun or moon but teaches that the sun is stone and the moon earth. Socrates then reminds Meletus that he was not the one who taught these things about the sun and moon. It was Anaxagoras the Clazomenian who stated that the sun and moon were only material substances. Meletus must have a very poor opinion of the judges at this trial if he thinks they will not be aware of his mistake. Furthermore, Socrates points out that Meletus has involved himself in a self-contradiction, since he accuses Socrates of introducing new and strange divinities and at the same time asserts that he is an atheist who does not believe in any god.

Having replied to the charges made by Meletus, Socrates proceeds to other matters related to his trial. The question has been raised as to whether it is proper for him to continue in a manner of living that could cause him to experience an untimely death? His answer is that he has no fear of death. Anyone in his circumstances ought not to calculate the chance of living or dying. He ought only to consider whether what he is doing is right or wrong. As a soldier in the army he did not desert his post when facing the danger of death. He would choose death in preference to disgrace, for it is better to die honorably than it is to live in dishonor. As he has explained before, his manner of living is in response to a command from God to fulfill the philosopher's mission of searching into himself and other men. Therefore, to disobey this command in order to save his own life would be a disgraceful thing to do. Addressing his hearers Socrates spoke the following words.

"If you say to me, Socrates this time we will not mind Anytus and will let you off, but on one condition, that you are not to inquire and speculate in this way any more, and if you are caught doing this again you will die. I will reply 'Men of Athens, I honor and love you; but I shall obey God rather than you, and while I have life and strength I shall never cease from the practice and teaching of philosophy, exhorting anyone whom I meet after my manner, and convincing him saying: O my friend, why do you, who are a citizen of the great and mighty and wise city of Athens, care so much about laying up the greatest amount of money and honor and reputation, and so little about wisdom and truth and the greatest improvement of the soul, you never regard or heed at all?' "

He concludes this part of his defense by saying, "For I do nothing but go about persuading you all, old and young alike, not to take thought for your persons or your properties but first and chiefly to care about the greatest improvement of the soul. This is my teaching, and if this is the doctrine which corrupts the youth, my influence is ruinous indeed. . . . Wherefore O men of Athens, I say to you, do as Anytus bids or not as Anytus bids, and either acquit me or not; but whatever you do, know that I shall never alter my ways, not even if I have to die many times." That he has not been guilty of corrupting the youth is evidenced by the fact that many of the ones who were associated with him years ago have now reached maturity and are therefore in a position to know if they have been corrupted. If that had been the case they would now be among his accusers. Instead, they are among his most devoted friends and loyal supporters. Socrates recognizes several of them in the audience before him.

Socrates is aware of the fact that persons who have been accused of some crime will often try to win sympathy for themselves or to influence their judges by bringing in members of their own families to plead in their behalf.

Socrates will not resort to any such tactics. He feels that conduct of that kind is discreditable both to himself and to the state. There is something wrong about petitioning a judge and thus procuring an acquittal instead of informing and convincing him. It is the duty of a judge, not to make a present of justice but to give judgment, for he has sworn that he will judge according to the laws and not according to his own good pleasure.

After the vote had been taken, Socrates expressed surprise that the size of the majority voting against him had not been larger than it was. Without the assistance of Meletus, Anytus, and Lycon, the opposition would not have amounted to more than a fifth of the votes and Socrates would have been acquitted. It was customary in Athens for a prisoner who had been condemned to death to have the opportunity of proposing an alternate sentence, which would be accepted if approved by a majority of the judges. The penalty might be changed to the payment of a sum of money, banishment from the city for a period of time, or a number of other things, any one of which would be preferable to a death sentence.

Socrates stated that he had no money with which to pay a fine, and although any one of a number of his friends would have been glad to supply him with whatever amount was needed, he could not accept it, for by so doing he would be admitting guilt of something about which he was entirely innocent. Neither was he willing to be exiled from the city in which he had always lived and where he had carried on his activities in obedience to a divine command. The only alternative to the death sentence that he proposed was that of being provided for at public expense in a manner that would be appropriate for one who has dedicated his life to the service and welfare of his fellow citizens. No more suitable reward could be offered a poor man who is a benefactor of the public and who desires leisure that he may use for the purpose of giving instruction.

It had been suggested that Socrates might escape the death penalty if he would cease carrying on the type of conversations that had aroused so much suspicion and controversy with reference to his activities. He would then be free to go to some foreign country and no one would interfere with what he was doing. Socrates replies to this suggestion by saying that it would be disobedience to a divine command for him to hold his tongue. He believes that the greatest good of man is daily to converse about virtue, examining both himself and others, for the unexamined life is not worth living. He has one favor to ask of his judges after he is gone. It is that they will be watchful of his sons when they have grown to manhood and punish them if they seem to care about riches, or anything more than virtue, or if they pretend to be something they are not.

Having finished with his defense, Socrates concludes with a final note of warning to those who have condemned him. They may think that because they have gotten rid of their troublemaker they will be at peace with

themselves and will be honored by those who come after them. This, however, is not what will happen. The truth is that in putting Socrates to death
they are harming themselves far more than they are doing harm to him.
That which one should regard as most important is not the avoidance of
death but rather the avoidance of unrighteousness.

This is what Socrates has to say. "And now, O men who have condemned me, I would fain prophesy to you; for I am about to die, and that
is the hour in which men are gifted with prophetic power. And I prophesy
to you who are my murderers, that immediately after my death punishment
far heavier than you have inflicted on me will surely await you. Me you have
killed because you wanted to escape the accuser, and not to give an account
of your lives. But that will not be as you suppose: far other wise. For I say
that there will be more accusers of you than there are now; accusers whom
hitherto I have restrained; and as they are younger they will be more severe
with you, and you will be more offended at them. For if you think that by
killing men you can avoid the accuser censuring your lives, you are mistaken; that is not a way of escape which is either possible or honorable; the
easiest and the noblest way is not to be crushing others, but to be improving
yourselves. This is the prophesy which I utter before my departure to the
judges who have condemned me."

Commentary

The *Apology* is in one sense a historical account of Socrates' defense of
himself at the time of his trial. It is generally believed to be the most reliable
record of the event that has been preserved. Nevertheless, we must bear in
mind that there are certain limitations necessarily involved in all historical
writing. History is never a complete and exact account of what has taken
place. It is always a record of what the historian believed to have taken
place. It is necessarily his interpretation of the event as it is viewed from the
perspective of the time and place of the writing. This does not mean that
the historical account is unreliable but only that it partakes of certain limitations that cannot be entirely avoided. In this particular instance, it allows
for the fact that Plato's conception of Socrates may be idealized to some
extent and it is quite possible that in some cases he may have reported what
he thinks ought to have been said rather than what Socrates did say. Even
so, after allowing for these limitations, we must recognize that Plato's understanding of Socrates and the manner of his defense is probably as close
to the actual facts as it is humanly possible for one to attain. This is indicated by a number of different facts. In the first place the *Apology* is the
one dialog in which Plato is referred to as one who was present at the trial.
This makes his writing the testimony of an eyewitness. Again, the account
appears to have been written shortly after the trial, in which case any inaccuracies or falsifications would have been detected by others who were

familiar with the circumstances. Finally, the account in the *Apology* is in harmony with the reports given by Xenophon and other writers and it is also consistent with references to the trial found in the other Platonic dialogs.

There is a bit of irony in Socrates' reference to the manner of his speech. The so-called rhetoricians of his day were noted for their eloquence, which usually consisted of an emotional appeal designed to win the approval of the audience rather than an attempt to make a clear presentation of the relevant facts. In claiming that he is not a rhetorician, Socrates wants to make it clear that he does not employ speech for the purpose of swaying the feelings of his audience. The only kind of rhetoric for which he has any use is that of making a presentation of facts in language so clear that all can understand.

Plato's purpose in writing this dialog included something more than a historical interest. He wanted to present Socrates in the role of a martyr, using that term in the very best sense of the word. It was the character of the man as seen from within that was especially noteworthy. In the case of Socrates, martyrdom was an exaltation, something more than an untimely death of one who had been treated unjustly. Here was a man who, in obedience to a divine command, had spent his life in devotion to the public good and who would not stoop to save his own life, if by so doing he would have to compromise with his own conscience.

In making his defense, Socrates says that he will reply to each of two kinds of accusation. The first one is general in character and has to do with much of the public opinion that has arisen in opposition to him. The second one is more specific and it seems quite probable that this is the one for which he has been indicted and brought to trial. The first one is related to the actual trial only in an indirect way. It is, however, necessary to deal with it at some length in order to prepare the way for a proper understanding of the case that is under consideration by the jury. It is also true that Socrates' reply to the first accusation throws a great deal of light on the situation as a whole, inasmuch as it reveals certain predominant traits of character of both the accuser and the accused.

As a result of Socrates' manner of living a number of popular stories had arisen concerning him. Some of them were of a humorous nature and were never intended to be taken seriously but were regarded as nothing more than a joke about some of his peculiarities. This seems to have been the case when Aristophanes caricatured him in the comedy called the *Clouds*. Socrates had accepted it as good fun and even appeared to be amused by it. Nevertheless, stories of this kind do have some effect on popular opinion and there are always some people who put a wrong interpretation on them. Other stories are of a more serious nature, in that they contain inaccuracies and are often confused with data that are entirely irrelevant to the activities of the person to whom they are attributed. This is what happened when Socrates was credited with certain doctrines that had been taught by Anaxagoras, the physical scientist. It had also been rumored that Socrates was one who charged fees for his instruction and was, therefore, interested in making money for himself. Socrates had no difficulty in replying to rumors of this type. He had never been interested in the physical sciences, although he was familiar with the theories of Anaxagoras. Anyone who was well informed would not have attributed theories about the sun and moon to Socrates, whose interests had always been along other lines. Certainly Meletus was foolish to suppose the judges would not be aware of his mistake. As to the rumor that Socrates charged fees for his instruction, any one of those who had listened to him could testify to the fact that he never made any charges for his services. In fact, he had good reasons for refusing to take money for what he was doing. He did not believe it was proper to place a money value on truth or the process of teaching people to think for themselves. Further than this, he did not want to exclude anyone from his services because they did not have the money to pay for them. Teaching people to improve themselves by learning how to think clearly and correctly was in his judgment the most valuable service that he could render, and he would have it available for all who would take advantage of it, regardless of their ability to pay, their social position, or any other consideration. This did not mean that he believed it was wrong for any teacher to charge for his instruction if he felt the need for so doing. Socrates even commended Evenus for charging so modest a rate of his pupils.

The story about the oracle of Delphi and the statement attributed to it concerning Socrates being the wisest man in Athens is another example of Socratic irony. Whether the story is to be regarded as literally true may be doubtful, but the purpose for which the story is used is clear enough. It was designed to expose the false claims of those who pretended to be something that they were not. Because the Athenians did not have an authoritative book comparable to the Bible for Christians and Jews or the Koran for the followers of Mohammed, it was customary to consult the local divinities concerning matters of importance that could not be settled by ordinary means. Except at Delphi there was no caste of priestly interpreters. In order to obtain answers to religious questions, intellectual Athenians would consult the popular poets, with their many stories having to do with the activities of the gods recognized by the state. Socrates did not accept these stories about the gods. One reason for rejecting them was the fact that the gods were credited with immoral acts of a type that would never be tolerated among human beings. Socrates believed the gods were good. He did not believe in the dark and disturbing legends that were being circulated about them. At any rate, he was distrustful of the poets and he had little if any faith in the local divinities, although he did take seriously the voice, or daemon, that would speak to him on certain occasions, telling him what not to do. Regardless of Socrates' personal convictions, the majority of Athenians did believe in the oracle of Delphi, and so it was possible to use this story as a means for exposing the false pretenses of those who claimed to have great wisdom but actually understood very little, if anything, concerning some of the most important problems pertaining to human life. The statement attributed to the oracle of Delphi could be made to harmonize with Socrates' admission of his own ignorance by pointing out that he was aware of his own ignorance, while those who claimed to be wise were not conscious of their own limitations.

Having dispensed with some of the false and idle rumors that had been in circulation concerning him and having exposed some of the false pretenses on the part of his accusers, Socrates proceeds to make his reply to the main charge that has led to his indictment. Meletus appears to be the chief prosecutor, although Anytus was in all likelihood the one who instigated the charge. They accused Socrates of being an evil person who does not believe in the gods of the state and who corrupts the youth by causing them to lose confidence in the government that has jurisdiction over them. Insofar as the charge against Socrates was that he did not believe in the gods recognized by the state, there can be no question about his being guilty. By his own admission, he did not accept many of the popular views concerning the Athenian gods, but this was by no means the only reason or even the main one for his being brought to trial. Although it was the stated reason for his indictment, the actual reason seems to have been the fact that his teachings were regarded as dangerous to those who were in positions of power. Athens was being ruled at this time by a democratic form of government, and if it could be made to appear that Socrates was an enemy of democracy this would go a long way toward arousing popular sentiment against him. It would indicate that his teachings might constitute a threat to the conventional standards and customs of the day.

In making his defense, Socrates did not attempt to prove that he was innocent of the charge of disbelief in the Athenian gods. Instead, he addressed himself to the larger implications involved in the so-called crimes of which he had been accused. So far as corrupting the youth was concerned, he made it plain that he had never attempted to indoctrinate his listeners or to coerce them into accepting a particular set of ideas. He did not claim to have arrived at the final or absolute truth himself nor did he insist that his pupils should hold the same views that he held. His only purpose was to stimulate and encourage each of them to think for himself. If that constituted a threat to the conventional standards and customs of the day, so be it. He was quite willing to accept responsibility for it. The charge that Socrates had corrupted the youth was based in part on the fact that some of the ones who had been associated with him had committed acts that were offensive to the state. This may have been true, for these persons were all free moral agents and, therefore, responsible for whatever they might do. Any misconduct on their part could not be attributed to Socrates. In fact, he was ready to summon the parents and elder brothers of the young men who have been associated with him as witnesses that none of them have been made worse by his companionship. Insofar as they have been influenced either by his teachings or his example, it has always been for the good.

That Socrates was a law-abiding citizen and not an enemy of the state is indicated by his conduct throughout his entire life. While serving as a soldier he remained at his post of duty under circumstances in which his own life was in great danger. Only on two occasions had his actions been in conflict with the constituted authorities of the land, and in both of these he had been commanded to do things that were either unconstitutional or in direct violation of the demands of justice. Although he believed the laws of God should be obeyed in preference to the laws of men, he never tried to escape the punishment demanded by the state for violation of laws that he believed to be unjust. He would not attempt to escape from prison in order to save his own life, even though he had ample opportunity to do so. He was not afraid to die. What he feared most of all was that he might do something that was morally wrong.

The opposition to Socrates on the part of Meletus and his associates was based to some extent on religious grounds. Because Socrates did not believe in the gods recognized by the state, it was inferred that he did not believe in any divine being. Meletus, in fact, when questioned about it, insists that Socrates is an atheist. The charge, of course, was a ridiculous one and Socrates makes this clear by pointing out that Meletus has contradicted himself by saying that Socrates has introduced new and strange divinities and yet does not believe in any deity. Actually, Socrates while not accepting many of the popular conceptions of religion, was a deeply religious person. He had a profound faith in the spiritual meaning of life and the world, along with a firm belief in God as the source of our moral obligations. Any prayer that he would address to the deity was never a plea for bodily comfort or material welfare but a petition for the humility and courage to live righteously under whatever circumstances might exist.

Socratic irony can be seen again in the argument to prove to Meletus that if Socrates had corrupted the youth it must have been done involuntarily and for that reason ought not to be punished. The reason given is that no one would voluntarily do harm to the people among whom he would have to live. The argument was a weak one even if it did reflect Socrates' belief that ignorance is the one thing that causes people to do wrong things. It was, however, an effective means of exposing the shallowness of Meletus' thinking and his inability to understand the logical implications of his own position.

As a further defense of his manner of living, Socrates mentions that he has avoided a political career because he believed it would have been futile for him to attempt any reform movement through a legislative process. Any attempt that he might make to remedy unfair conditions would arouse the antagonism of those who were gaining material benefits from these practices and they would put an end to his career. As a public official, in order for him to fight for what he believed was right, he would have been opposed by the many, who would put him to death and thus make it impossible for him to do any good. This had been the experience of many good persons in the past and in this respect he did not think conditions had changed. Twice in his own lifetime he had fought for the cause of justice in opposition to popular demand and in both instances he had done so at the risk of his own life. When told that it might still be possible for him to save his life if he would agree to change his manner of living and stop talking to people about controversial issues, Socrates replies that death is not necessarily an evil thing. There are certain advantages to be gained by it and while he has no positive assurance of a life after death there is a possibility of continued existence under conditions that are far more pleasant than the ones that are now being experienced. Furthermore, his manner of living has been in obedience to a divine command and for this reason he would, if given the opportunity, continue to preach to all men of all ages the necessity of virtue and improvement, even if a thousand deaths should await him.

It is quite possible that Socrates' judges did not really desire his execution, inasmuch as that would place the responsibility for his death on their hands. Evidently, they expected him to take advantage of the opportunity to propose an alternative sentence, such as the payment of a fine or banishment from the city. A proposal of this kind would enable him to escape the death sentence and at the same time provide some justification for the verdict they had rendered. The alternative sentence that Socrates did propose was so contrary to what the judges had expected that it might seem to have been made for the purpose of irritating them. Although he probably had no idea that his proposal would be accepted, Socrates explained his reasons for making it. Since it was generally understood that the function of the court was to make justice prevail, nothing less than what he had proposed would be a just compensation for his lifelong services to the state.

Evidence that Socrates was sincere in his professed loyalty to the cause of justice can be seen from the way in which he has conducted himself throughout the entire course of his life. The favor he asks of the judges to watch over his sons after he has gone and they have grown to manhood is in keeping with his devotion to what he believes is right. He wants his sons to follow the path of virtue as he has done, and so he asks that if they should seem to care about riches or anything more than virtue, or if they should pretend to be something they are not, measures should be taken to correct them. Again, it was his desire to do nothing that would hinder the cause of justice that led him to dismiss the members of his own family, so that their presence would not cause the judges to be moved by feelings of sympathy and pity in place of reasoned judgment.

The *Apology* ends with the speech in which Socrates utters a prophetic warning to his judges concerning the verdict that history will pronounce upon them for the actions they have taken in condemning him to death. It is a remarkable speech and one that illustrates Socrates' deep conviction that it is far better to suffer injustice than it is to practice injustice. What one needs to fear most of all is not what happens to one's body but what happens to his soul. Injustice may appear to be triumphant at the time but eventually evildoers will be given a just recompense. Whether this speech was actually given by Socrates at the time of his trial or is merely one that Plato believed would have been appropriate for him to give at that time is a question that cannot be answered with certainty. If the *Apology* was written shortly after the death of Socrates as we have good reasons for believing, the prophetic warning had not been fulfilled at that time, nor was it accomplished during the years that immediately followed. It is, however, quite possible that either Plato or Socrates had in mind the distant future and certainly from the long-range point of view the prophecy has been abundantly fulfilled. For many generations Socrates has been regarded as a hero and classified with those individuals whose martyrdom has contributed much to the cause of freedom and justice in the world. His place in history is indicated by the following lines from the pen of William W. Story.

> Speak history—Who are life's victors
> Unroll thy long annals and say
> Are those whom the world called victors
> Who won the success of a day
> The martyrs or Nero
> The Spartans who fell at Thermopylae's tryst
> Or the Persians and Xerxes
> His judges or Socrates, Nero or Paul, Caesar or Christ.

CRITO

Summary

The *Crito* records the conversation that took place in the prison where Socrates was confined awaiting his execution. It is in the form of a dialog between Socrates and Crito, an elderly Athenian who for many years has been a devoted friend of Socrates and a firm believer in his ethical teachings. The conversation takes place at an early hour on what proved to be the next-to-the-last day that Socrates remained alive. Like both the *Euthyphro* and the *Apology,* this dialog reveals something of the character of Socrates by describing the manner in which he faced difficult circumstances without being overcome by them. In the *Crito* particular attention is given to the reasons advanced by Socrates for refusing to escape from prison as a means of saving his own life. The circumstances were such that he might easily have done so and his friends were urging him to do it.

The dialog begins with Socrates asking Crito why he has arrived at so early an hour. The dawn is just beginning to break and Socrates has been sleeping soundly throughout the night. Crito explains that he has been waiting in the prison for some little time but has remained silent because he did not want to disturb Socrates' sleep. He adds that he is astonished to find that Socrates has been able to sleep so well and to remain calm and peaceful when the time for his execution is so close at hand. Socrates has been in prison for about a month, owing to the fact that no execution of a criminal would be allowed in the city until a certain ship has returned from the island of Delos. Crito reports that the ship is soon to arrive, for he has been told that it has left Sunium and is expected to be in Athens the next day. For this reason, Crito tells Socrates that tomorrow will be his last day alive. Socrates states that if such is the will of God he is willing to die. However, he is convinced, because of a dream that he experienced that morning, that there will be a delay of one more day.

At this point Crito pleads with Socrates to take his advice and escape from prison. He gives as his reason that if Socrates refuses to escape and is then put to death, Crito will not only have lost a true friend who can never be replaced but he will also be censured by many persons, who will accuse him of failure to do what he could in order to save the life of a friend. It will be supposed by those who are not familiar with the facts that Crito could have purchased the freedom of his friend by paying a certain amount of money but that he refused to do so. Hence, if Socrates cares about the reputation of his friend in the future he will act in accordance with the request that that friend is now making of him. Socrates must admit that the opinion of the majority is something that cannot be ignored, for they are capable of inflicting great harm on anyone who has incurred their disapproval.

Socrates is not concerned about the opinion of the majority, for it is capable of neither the greatest evil nor the greatest good. It cannot make a man wise and it cannot make one foolish. Whatever it does is largely a matter of chance. Crito asks if Socrates does not fear that escaping from prison would cause his friends to get in trouble with the authorities of the land and that this might cause them to lose a portion of their property or possibly suffer something that might be even worse than that? Socrates admits that he does have that fear but it is by no means the only one that he has. Crito then tells him to have no such fear, for there are persons who at no great cost are willing to save him and bring him out of prison. As for the informers, they are far from being exorbitant in their demands and a little money will satisfy them. Crito explains that he has considerable means himself, all of which he would gladly use for any purpose that would aid in saving the life of Socrates. Furthermore, if Socrates should feel hesitant about allowing Crito to spend so much in his behalf, there are many more of his friends who are ready and willing to supply whatever amount of money is needed for this purpose.

If these offers of assistance are not sufficient to persuade Socrates to attempt an escape from prison, Crito presents some additional reasons in support of what he has been urging him to do. He tells him that by remaining in prison and refusing to escape he is playing into the hands of his enemies and giving aid to the ones who are disregarding the demands of justice. Then, too, he is betraying the members of his own family, especially the children, who are entitled to the nurture, guidance, and education that he could provide by staying alive and doing what is within his power for their welfare. If, Crito says, instead of fulfilling your obligations to them, you go away and leave them to take their chances amid all the unfortunate circumstances that may arise, you cannot be held blameless if they should fall into evil ways. This is not the kind of action that is appropriate for one who professes, as you do, to be following the course of virtue. By refusing to escape, you will be taking the easier but not the better and manlier part and, therefore, people will be ashamed not only of you but also of your friends, who they will maintain were lacking in the necessary courage to save you from an untimely death.

In reply to what Crito has been saying, Socrates admits that his zeal is invaluable if it is used in support of what is right, but if used in support of what is wrong it leads to an even greater evil. Throughout his entire life Socrates has made it a point not to be swayed by emotional appeals but to follow a course that is directed by reason. Therefore, he will not forsake the principles that he has honored for a long time but will remain true to whatever reason tells him is demanded by them. The arguments advanced by Crito have not convinced him that he should escape from prison and he proceeds to set forth the reasons for rejecting them.

Crito has mentioned that, in the opinion of many persons, both Socrates and his friends will be severely criticized if he fails to make any attempt to escape from prison. Socrates, in reply, calls attention to the danger that is involved in following public opinion. He asks if it is not true that the opinion of some persons should be regarded and the opinion of others be disregarded. After Crito has admitted that this is true, the question is raised concerning whose opinion should be regarded seriously enough to be followed? To answer this question, Socrates suggests an analogous situation. In the case of one who is being trained in gymnastics, whose opinion should be sought in regard to praise or blame for what he is doing? Is it the opinion of the many or of the one who is his instructor or trainer? When a person is seriously ill is it proper to ask the opinion of the many or the one who is a qualified physician? Obviously, it is the opinion of the one person who possesses the necessary relevant information that should be followed. If this is true in regard to physical exercise and matters pertaining to health, is it not even more important to consult the opinion of those who have an adequate understanding about what is just and unjust, fair and foul, or good and evil? If, acting on the advice of men who have no understanding we injure the body, is it not true that we will incur an even greater evil by following the advice of those who have no proper understanding of the meaning of justice and that which pertains to that part of human nature that is superior to the body?

Crito is forced to admit that Socrates has presented a strong argument with reference to the inadvisability of following public opinion, or even the voice of the majority, when it comes to matters of crucial importance. Nevertheless, Crito still insists that the opinion of the many is not something to be neglected entirely, for the simple reason that the many possess the power to put people to death, and to save one's own life is more important than anything else he can do. Socrates does not agree that one should save his own life at any cost. He holds that it is not life but a good life that is to be valued above everything else. He believes, too, that a good life is equivalent to one that is just and honorable. The other considerations that Crito has mentioned, such as money, the loss of a good reputation, and the duty of educating one's children are only the doctrines of the multitude. They are not to be accepted just because they express the opinions of the majority but are to be followed only in those instances where they are supported by good reasons. From this it follows that the question confronting Crito and Socrates is whether it is right and honorable for one who has been put in prison by the constituted authorities to escape or to allow others to aid him in so doing by the use of money or any other unlawful means.

Both Socrates and Crito have admitted on previous occasions that one should never intentionally do what is wrong and now they must decide if they are to abide by that principle or depart from it. If they do abide by it they must admit that it would be wrong for Socrates to heed the advice of Crito by trying to escape from prison. An escape would be a violation of the law of the land and this would imply that Socrates is an enemy of that which makes for an orderly society. He cannot do this without going back on the principles for which he has stood throughout his entire life. Still, Crito is not convinced, for he maintains that Socrates has been the victim of unjust laws and for this reason it is proper and right for him to disobey them. Socrates then reminds him that to act in that manner would be a case of returning evil for evil and this would contradict what he has already admitted should never be done. To return evil for evil may be in harmony with the morality of the many, but as he has indicated before, public opinion when it is not supported by good reasons is never a safe guide to follow.

Crito is of the opinion that it would not be wrong for Socrates to escape because he has been imprisoned unjustly. Socrates does not agree with him and, accordingly, he sets forth his reasons for holding that one is obliged to submit to the punishment imposed on him, even though the punishment may be an unjust one. His argument is based on the fact that he is a citizen of the state, having been born, nourished, and educated within its borders. In fact, he is a child of the state and has an obligation toward it similar to that of a child to its parents. By living in the state for these many years and accepting the benefits it has provided, he has indicated a willingness to accept its laws and regulations and to abide by the decisions of its courts, regardless of what those decisions might be.

Socrates asks Crito to consider for a moment what the officials of the government might say to him under the existing circumstances. They might say something like the following. "There is clear proof Socrates that we and the city were not displeasing to you. Of all Athenians you have been the most constant resident in the city, which, as you never leave, you may be supposed to love. . . . and you acquiesced in our government of you; and this is the state in which you begat your children, which is a proof of your satisfaction. Moreover, you might, if you had liked, have fixed the penalty at banishment in the course of the trial—the state which refuses to let you go now would have let you go then. But you pretended that you preferred death to exile, and that you were not grieved at death. And now you have forgotten these fine sentiments, and pay no respect to us the laws, of whom you are the destroyer; and are doing only what a miserable slave would do, running away and turning your back upon the compacts and agreements which you made as a citizen. . . . Are we not right in saying that you agreed to be governed according to us in deed, and not in word only?"

Crito admits there is no adequate reply to an argument of this type on the part of the state and he continues to listen as Socrates develops still further the charges that could be brought against him in the event that he should escape. They could say that he has broken the covenants and agreements he made with them, not in haste or on the spur of the moment, but in times of leisure without any deception or compulsion on their part. He has had seventy years to think it over and during this time he was free to leave the city and go to any of those places that he praised for their good government, but instead of doing this, he chose to remain in our city and to abide by its laws.

If under the circumstances that have just been pointed out, Socrates should escape from prison it would be of no benefit either to him or to his friends. Those who were known to have aided him in making his escape would be driven into exile, or lose their property and be deprived of citizenship. If he should go to one of the neighboring cities, such as Thebes or

Megara, he would be regarded as an enemy and all of their patriotic citizens would look upon him as a subverter of the laws. In addition, they would argue that anyone who is a subverter of the laws would also be a corrupter of the young and foolish portion of mankind. If Socrates should go away from well-governed states to Crito's friends in Thessaly, his reception there would be no better, for the people would ridicule him for preaching lofty sentiments about justice and virtue and then betraying all that he has taught in order to gain a little longer life.

By refusing to escape, Socrates can depart from this life in innocence, a sufferer and not a doer of evil, and a victim, not of the laws but of men. On the other hand, if he goes forth returning evil for evil, and injury for injury, breaking the covenants and agreements he has made, the citizens of the state, including his own friends, will despise him and look upon him as an enemy who has done his best to destroy them. All of this, Socrates tells Crito, is the voice that he seems to hear murmuring in his ears and that prevents him from hearing anything else. He then tells Crito to speak if he has anything to say in reply to what has been said. Since Crito has nothing more to say. Socrates asks that he be allowed to follow the intimations of the will of God.

Commentary

In common with the *Euthyphro* and the *Apology,* the *Crito* has to do with the character of Socrates. He has been portrayed as a religious man who has spent the greater portion of his life in obedience to what he regarded as a divine command. The mysterious voice to which he always paid attention was to him the voice of God. Acting in harmony with this voice, he was accustomed to do what he believed was right and he would not depart from this course in order to save his own life. This was made clear in both the *Euthyphro* and the *Apology,* but one question remained and it forms the chief topic of conversation in the *Crito*. The question was whether or not one is morally obligated to obey laws that are believed to be unjust? In the case of Socrates, there was ample evidence to indicate he had been condemned unjustly and that the law that demanded his execution was not a good one. Under these circumstances, would it be wrong for Socrates to escape from prison in violation of the law that had placed him there? Crito, along with other friends of Socrates, believes he would be amply justified in breaking this law and a number of arguments are presented in support of that belief. Socrates is convinced they are wrong in holding that opinion, and he proceeds at some length to set forth his reasons for rejecting the view that they have presented.

The issue raised in this dialog is an important one, for it has given rise to controversies that have persisted over the centuries and in certain areas it is still an issue at the present time. Ought one to accept the penalty imposed on him by legal means that are unjust? Evidently, Plato's purpose in writing this dialog involved something more than a historical account of the conversation that took place in Socrates' prison shortly before his death. He wanted to deal with the moral issue involved in those situations where individuals are confronted with penalties imposed on them by unjust laws. One point that has frequently been overlooked is the distinction between what is moral and what is legal. It is this point that the dialog is intended to clarify. It is simply not true that all laws should be obeyed under any and all conditions. This is indicated when Socrates admits that on two occasions he violated the laws of the city and he makes no apology for doing so in either instance. He has stated on different occasions that he will obey God rather than man, and this means that he will not violate the demands of his own conscience in order to do what the state has ordered him to do. Why then should he refuse to escape prison just because the law requires him to remain there? The answer is that, although one may violate the laws of the land in order to satisfy the demands of his conscience, he has the moral obligation to accept the penalty for the violation of those laws that is imposed by the state. To do otherwise would mean a repudiation of the system of law and order that makes living in a civilized society possible.

The conversation between Crito and Socrates takes place in the early hours of the morning. Socrates has been sleeping soundly, in spite of the fact that he knows the time for his execution is close at hand. The calm and quiet manner with which Socrates accepts his fate astonishes his visitor, but it is only one more illustration of the extent to which Socrates has achieved control of his feelings and emotions. He has always insisted that the good life is one in which the individual's activities are governed by reason and not by the feelings of the moment. His teaching in this respect is imparted as much by his example as by anything he says. The date for Socrates' execution has been delayed for about a month, pending the return of the ship from the island of Delos. The brief reference to his dream is an example of the popular belief that events may be foretold in that manner. In this instance it proved to be correct. Crito explained that his coming at so early an hour was due to his belief that the time was short and if any action was to be taken it must be done at once. Socrates informs him that it will require one more day for the ship to reach Athens and they will have plenty of time to discuss whatever it is that Crito has in mind. Crito has come for the purpose of pleading with Socrates to escape from prison. He has a number of reasons for believing this is what Socrates should do, and he hopes that by setting forth these reasons he can convince Socrates that it is not only morally right but the part of wisdom for him to act as Crito is urging him to do.

One reason that Crito advances is based chiefly on what he anticipates people will say in the event that Socrates remains in prison and is put to death. They will say that his friend Crito might have saved him if he had been willing to furnish the money to purchase his freedom. Such accusations could only add to the grief that Crito would already have experienced in the loss of a friend who could never be replaced. Crito has stated that he would gladly give all the money he has if by so doing he could secure Socrates' freedom, and if that should prove to be not enough, he knows of several friends who would likewise contribute whatever was necessary to accomplish this purpose. But there are other reasons, too, why Crito believes that Socrates should escape. The court that had condemned him was not a competent court. Their understanding was not sufficient to enable them to determine if Socrates was really a corrupter of the youth. Their judgment was not a correct one and, therefore, Socrates is under no obligation to see that it is carried out. Again, Crito maintains that it is proper and right to return evil for evil. Because Socrates has been treated in an evil manner, it will be only a matter of justice for him to treat the state in a like manner. To support his position still further, Crito points out that by refusing to escape from prison Socrates will be inflicting a great hardship on the members of his own family. He has no right to bring children into the world and then fail to provide them with the nurture and education to which they are entitled. Finally, Crito mentions that in case Socrates should leave Athens and go into exile there are good prospects for his being well received. Crito has friends in Thessaly, and Socrates could live among them in peace, with no fears that the inhabitants of that place would ever cause him any trouble. If Socrates is hesitant about making his escape because he fears that such an action on his part would get his friends into trouble, Crito reminds him that he need have no such fear, for with a small amount of money that his friends would be happy to contribute, they could buy off the informers who would report to the authorities concerning his escape.

In reply to what Crito has been saying, Socrates expresses his appreciation for the friendship and goodwill that have been displayed and for the zeal that has been manifested in their presentation. Still, Socrates is not convinced that he should escape from prison or that it would be morally right for him to attempt any such action. He has listened carefully to Crito's arguments and will state his reasons for objecting to each of them. Crito is wrong in allowing the opinion of the many to influence his judgment. Socrates tells him that it is not the opinion of the majority that is most important but rather the opinion of the ones who have an adequate understanding of the issue that is involved. It is true that in a democracy it is the will of the majority that is supposed to prevail, but neither Socrates nor Plato believe in democracy so long as it is interpreted to mean that the opinion of ignorant persons is to be given equal weight with the opinion of those who are well informed. They do, however, believe in the democratic principle that in the administration of the laws all persons should be treated alike. No discrimination based on wealth or social position should be permitted. With regard to the rightness of an escape from prison, the situation is analogous to that of one who is being trained in gymnastics or one who is physically ill. It is not the opinion of the majority that should be consulted but rather the opinion of the trainer in one case and that of the qualified physician in the other. Crito should be reminded that it is only the opinion of those who have a clear understanding of what is right and wrong that should influence his decision.

Socrates does not deny that he has been treated unjustly by the court and neither does he think that the judges who condemned him were competent to determine the correctness of his religious views or to decide whether he had really been a corrupter of the youth. He does not agree with Crito that these facts are sufficient to make it right for him to escape prison by violating the law that has been prescribed. The issue that is raised in this connection has been a controversial one and it is by no means clear that the intellectual Greeks of Socrates' day would have agreed with him. We do know that, after the death of Socrates, Plato did leave Athens because he did not think it would be safe for him to remain there. At a later date, Plato's pupil Aristotle left Athens to escape death at the hands of the anti-Macedonians, saying that he wanted to spare the city from another crime against philosophy. It has been suggested by some Greek scholars that Plato might have escaped from prison if he had been in Socrates' position. We cannot be certain about what he would have done under these circumstances, but there is one important difference between Plato and Socrates at the time when the conversation with Crito took place. The difference is that Socrates was seventy years old, while Plato was only a young man in his early thirties. Socrates had spent his entire life in Athens. During all of those years, he had been the recipient of the many benefits that the city bestowed and he had often acknowledged his indebtedness to its system of government and social order. If he had chosen to do so, he could have left the city at any time but his very presence and participation in the life of the city was evidence of his approval of the way in which its activities had been maintained. Plato was at this time too young to have been under the same or equal obligation to the state, inasmuch as he had not received as much from it. His situation was quite different from that of an old man who had lived during those years when the Periclean Age was at its greatest height of achievement. Socrates could not go back on his obligations to the city, and unless commanded to do that which in his judgment was morally wrong, he was duty-bound to obey its laws.

Crito had urged Socrates to return evil for evil. This was a principle accepted by the many, presumably on the assumption that only in this way could the demands of justice be met. No one questioned the idea that criminals should be punished or that the severity of the punishment should be determined to some extent by the nature of the crime. There was, however, a difference of opinion concerning the purpose of the punishment. According to one view, its purpose was to serve as a corrective measure that would be of benefit to the criminal by helping him to overcome his evil tendencies. A quite different view was held by those who believed that the proper function of punishment was to enable society to get even with the criminal by inflicting upon him an evil that was equivalent to the one he had caused others to suffer. Socrates accepted the former of these two views but rejected the latter. He did not believe that two wrongs make a right or that you can cure one evil by committing another one. Therefore, an escape from prison in violation of the law would be an evil act on his part and in no way would it counteract the evil performed by the court. Although Socrates lived and died several centuries before the Christian era, his position in this respect was similar to what later came to be known as the Christian view, which forbids one to overcome evil with evil but states rather that evil should be overcome with good.

Crito has said that the opinion of the many should be feared because they have the power to put people to death. Socrates is not disturbed by this fact, for he believes that death is not necessarily an evil thing. It is the committing of an evil act that should be feared rather than having to die. The many may think that it is within their power to do the greatest evil to one who has lost their good favor but such is not the case. They cannot make a person wise or foolish, nor can they cause him to do good or evil. It is true that they may injure one's body and they may even be the cause of one's physical death but they have no power over his soul and that is what really matters. What Socrates believed in this respect was identical with what the Christians of later centuries taught when they said "Be not afraid of them that kill the body, and after that have no more that they can do." Socrates emphasized the point that the soul is made better by doing what is right and is made worse by doing what is wrong and it was his conviction that the element in each individual in which wickedness and righteousness have their seat is far more precious than the physical body.

Crito and Socrates have been able to discuss the question about making an escape from prison because they have agreed on certain points. They both believe that to commit a wrong is under all conditions a bad thing for the man who commits it. From this it follows that a man must never repay ill-treatment by ill-treatment and no treatment received from another ever justifies doing something wrong in return. If they did not believe alike on these points any discussion of the question would be useless. Socrates has made an effective reply to the arguments advanced by Crito, stating at some length his reasons for believing that it would be wrong for him to escape. Still, Crito insists that he has not changed his mind and Socrates decides to try a different approach to the question.

He will relate what he imagines the many, or people in general, will say if he does escape from prison and go to some foreign land to spend the remainder of his life. This might seem at first to be a strange thing for Socrates to do, in view of all that he has said concerning the shallowness of the opinions of the many. But, in this case, he will attempt to relate not simply what they might say but rather what they would have a right to say in the event that he escaped. The opinion of the many is not necessarily wrong and neither is it necessarily right. It can be right if it is based on actual facts and what can logically be inferred from them. This is what Socrates intends to present as he makes his final speech in defense of the position he has taken.

Let us consider, he says, what the State or the Laws would have to say in the event they should discover Socrates making his escape from prison. This personification of the State, or what is sometimes referred to as the Laws, is an artistic device that brings home to the imagination in a powerful way the message that Socrates has been trying to convey. It does not contain any additional argument to what has been said before but it is designed to produce a mood of feeling that is appropriate for an elevation of the ethical demands of conscience. Its purpose is to arouse an unconditional reverence for the dignity of the moral law that demands and justifies the course that Socrates is taking. The basis for the remarks that follow is the "social contract" that exists between the individual citizen and the society to which he belongs. It is this contract, or implied agreement, in which the citizen promises to obey the laws of the state and to abide by the decisions of its courts that makes possible a well-ordered society in which people can live at peace with one another.

If Socrates should follow the advice of Crito and escape from prison, the Laws might complain that he is breaking the contract that he made with them. Since the contract was made voluntarily, he cannot offer the excuse that it was made under duress or obtained by false representation. Neither was it made in haste without sufficient time for consideration. Socrates has had seventy years for reflection and in all this time he has not left the city in search of a different place to live. His choice of living under the laws of this city has been free and deliberate. His entire life bears witness to the fact that he has accepted the institutions of the society into which he was born, and it is an essential part of the system under which that society operates that its citizens shall respect and obey the decisions of its duly constituted courts. Socrates is not at liberty to reject the decisions of the court because he believes they have gone beyond their jurisdiction or that they have made a wrong decision in his case. For him to run away in order to escape the execution of the court's sentence would not only be a dishonorable act but it would indicate an insincerity on his part, since he is not willing to abide by the lofty ideals that have characterized his teachings.

If Socrates should escape, his family and friends will run the risk of banishment and loss of property. If he goes to neighboring cities, he will be looked upon by all honest citizens as an enemy. Even if he should escape that disgrace, he will be regarded as a parasite, or one who is seeking favors from the rich and the powerful. He will be ashamed to continue his professions of devotion to goodness with conduct of this kind staring him in the face. On the other hand, if he refuses to escape from prison and abides by the execution of the sentence pronounced upon him, he will have a good defense when he stands before the tribunal of the judgment of the dead. Before them, he will appear as an innocent victim of the injustice, not of law, but of those who have abused the law in order to bring about his destruction.

It is this appeal that Socrates finds ringing in his ears. It makes him deaf to the pleadings of Crito, who now finds that he has nothing more to say. Therefore, Socrates feels content to follow the path along which God has been leading him.

PHAEDO

Summary

After an interval of some months or years an account of the last hours of Socrates is narrated to Echecrates and other interested persons by Phaedo, a beloved disciple of the great teacher. The narration takes place at Phlius, a town of Sicyon. The dialog takes the form of a narrative because Socrates is described acting as well as speaking, and the particulars of the event are interesting to distant friends as well as to the narrator himself. Phaedo is asked if he had been present with Socrates on the day that he drank the poison. He replies that he was present and he also mentions several of the other persons who were there at the time. These included Simmias, Cebes, Crito, Apollodorus, and several other people. Plato was not present at this meeting, having been kept away because of illness.

The chief topic of conversation had been Socrates' conception of the soul. Inasmuch as all of those present were aware of the fact that Socrates would be put to death that day, they wanted to know what their beloved teacher believed concerning the nature of the soul. There were many questions that they would like to have answered. They included such items as the following. What assurance or proof do we have that souls actually exist? How is the soul related to the body? What happens to the soul at the time of death; does it disintegrate into nothingness or does it continue to exist in some form? Are souls immortal in the sense that they have neither a beginning nor an end? Are souls influenced by contact with the body? Are there both good and bad souls, and if so, what constitutes the difference between them? Are souls either punished or rewarded in some future life?

These questions, along with others closely related to them, are discussed at some length as Socrates attempts to present his ideas in a manner that is both clear and convincing.

The dialog begins with a request that Phaedo report to the group of visitors about the death of Socrates, telling them what he had to say during his last hours. Some of those who were present had heard that Socrates had been condemned to drink poison but they knew very little about it and were anxious to learn more of the details. Phaedo explained the reason why the execution had been delayed for a month, pending the return of the ship from the island of Delos. He also described something of his own feelings as he witnessed the death of his very dear friend. He did not pity Socrates, for his mien and his language were so noble and fearless in the hour of death that he appeared to be blessed.

After having mentioned the names of several of those who were present at the time of Socrates' death, Phaedo states that he will endeavor to repeat the entire conversation as he remembers the way in which it took place. As the group entered the prison on the morning of Socrates' last day, they observed that he had just been released from chains. His wife, Xanthippe, was sitting by him, holding their child in her arms. She was weeping because this was the last time she could converse with her husband. Socrates turned to Crito and asked that he have someone take her home. After this had been done and some remarks had been made concerning the readiness with which a true philosopher would approach death, Cebes asks Socrates why it is that he believes it is wrong for one to commit suicide, since death is not something to be feared?

Socrates admits there is an apparent inconsistency in his position but a careful consideration of the problem will reveal there is no real inconsistency. The reason is that we as human beings are in the hands of the gods. They are our guardians and we are their possessions. Since we belong to the gods, it is wrong for us to destroy their possessions, except in those instances that are in accordance with their will. Neither Cebes nor Simmias are satisfied with this statement and Socrates proceeds to give additional reasons in support of his position. Although he believes that suicide is wrong, he has no fear of death so long as he is acting in harmony with the will of God. He would be grieved at death if he did not believe the soul would fare better after death than when it is dwelling in the body. He is convinced, however, that after the soul is separated from the body it will go to other gods and will be associated with the souls of departed men who are even better than those now living on the earth. Socrates admits that he has no positive proof of this but he believes it to be true and he is aware of no facts to indicate the contrary.

At this point, Crito interrupts the conversation to inform them that the jailer has requested Socrates not to talk so much lest the heat generated by his talking might interfere with the action of the poison he must take and thereby make it necessary to have it administered more than once. Socrates instructs Crito to tell the jailer to mind his own business and be prepared to give the poison as many times as is required.

Following this brief interruption, Socrates enters into a discussion with Cebes and Simmias concerning the nature of death. He says, "And now I will make answer to you, O my judges, and show that he who has lived as a true philosopher has reason to be of good cheer when he is about to die, and that after death he may hope to receive the greatest good in the other world. . . . For I deem that the true discipline of philosophy is likely to be misunderstood by other men; they do not perceive that he is ever pursuing death and dying; and if this is true, why, having had the desire of death all his life long, should he repine at the arrival of that which he has been always pursuing and desiring?" Death, he explains, is nothing more than the separation of soul and body. Now, a true philosopher is one who ought not to place the highest value on the pleasures of the body, such as eating and drinking or the acquisition of costly raiment. He cares for these things only to the extent that they are necessary to meet nature's needs. His primary concern is for the soul, and for this reason, he would like to be rid of the body, insofar as it interferes with the welfare of the soul. It is true that the rest of the world are of the opinion that apart from bodily pleasures life is not worth living but in this respect they are mistaken. The philosopher knows that the soul is superior to the body and should be its master rather than its slave.

As the body desires pleasures of the flesh, so the soul desires wisdom. The pleasures of the body are experienced through the senses but the acquisition of wisdom comes only through the intellect. Truth cannot be perceived by the senses and so long as the search for final and absolute truth is accompanied by one's body he is bound to be deceived. True existence, if it is revealed at all, must come through the processes of thought, and thought functions at its best when the mind is no longer troubled by sounds or sights or pains or pleasures. It must have as little as possible to do with the body as it aspires to wisdom and a knowledge of ultimate reality. It is in this respect that the philosopher dishonors the body, for his soul runs away from the body and desires to be alone and by itself.

Socrates continued his argument by calling attention to the fact that justice, beauty, and goodness in their final, or absolute, form have never been perceived by the eyes, ears, or any other bodily sense. Anyone who attains to a knowledge of them in their highest purity must do so through the mind alone, without the distraction of sight, sound, or any other sense. From this we must conclude that, so long as we are in the body and the soul is mixed with this evil, our desire for the truth will not be satisfied. The body is a source of endless trouble by reason of its requirements of food, its liability to diseases, and filling our lives with loves, lusts, and fears. "For whence come wars, and fighting, and factions? . . . For wars are occasioned by the love of money, and money has to be acquired for the sake and in the service of the body; and in consequence of all these things the time which ought to be given to philosophy is lost." He concludes this part of the argument by pointing out that after death the foolishness of the body will have been cleared away and we shall be pure and hold converse with other pure souls and we will possess the light of truth. If this be true it would be most absurd for one who is a lover of wisdom to be fearful of death. Whenever you see a man who is repining at the approach of death you may be sure this is sufficient proof that he is not a lover of wisdom but a lover of the body and probably at the same time a lover of money or of power.

Cebes has been deeply impressed by what Socrates has said concerning the advantages to be gained by a separation of the soul from the body. He is in agreement with most of the argument but he questions the premise on which much of it is based. He is not convinced that there are sufficient reasons for believing in the continued existence of the soul following the death of the body. He thinks it quite possible that upon its release from the body the soul may disintegrate and like smoke or air vanish into nothingness. If Socrates has more arguments to support his belief that when a man is dead his soul still exists, having force or intelligence, he would like to hear them. So far as his present opinion is concerned, Cebes remains skeptical.

In response to this skeptical attitude on the part of Cebes, Socrates makes some reference to the Heraclitean doctrine of the strife of opposites. According to this conception, the world is in a constant state of flux. Everything is constantly changing into its opposite. Day changes into night and night changes into day. Life changes into death and death changes into life. All things that have opposites are generated out of their opposites. This is a principle that holds true universally. Anything that becomes greater must become greater after being less and that which becomes less must have been once greater and then become less. The weaker is generated from the stronger and the swifter from the slower. This holds of all opposites. They are generated out of one another and there is a passing or process from one to the other of them.

Life and death are opposites just as sleep and waking are opposites. Out of sleeping, waking is generated and the process of generation is in the one case falling asleep and in the other waking up. By the same type of analysis, we may say that death is generated from life and life is generated from death. Since the living come from the dead and the dead come from the living, it follows that the souls of the dead must be in some place out of which they come again. Furthermore, we must recognize that if all things that partake of life were to die and after they were dead remained in the form of death and did not come to life again, all would at last die and nothing would be alive. Cebes admits at this point he is now convinced that the souls of the dead are in existence and what happens to the good souls is different from that of the evil souls. He believes, too, that the doctrine of reminiscence offers further proof of the thesis that Socrates has been expounding. Simmias then asks for a further explanation of what this doctrine about recollection really means.

Cebes remarks that one proof of the recollection theory can be established simply by asking questions. By having the proper questions put to him in the right manner, a person will be able to answer correctly about something of which he was totally unaware before the questions were asked. He would be unable to do this if the knowledge had not in some sense been present within him. The questions that were asked served the purpose of stimulating the mind, so that it was able to recall that which had been known at some previous time. It might be that this knowledge had been gained by the soul during its existence in some prior embodiment.

Socrates then adds some further remarks to strengthen the argument in support of the recollection doctrine. He asks if there is such a thing as equality? He does not mean equality of one piece of wood with another or of one stone with another but equality in the abstract, or apart from its application to particular things. He means absolute equality. Both Cebes and Simmias agree that there is such a thing. Socrates then points out that equality in this sense cannot be perceived by the senses. Two things may appear to us to be equal to each other but there will always be some difference between them. Perfect or absolute equality does not exist in the world of our sense experience. How then is it possible for us to know anything about this type of equality, which has never been experienced by any of our senses? Clearly, the idea of equality in its pure state must have been acquired at some time previous to birth. From this it follows that from the moment of our birth we have been in possession of this knowledge, and this is true not only for the idea of equality but of other ideas, such as justice, truth, beauty, and goodness. But if this knowledge, which we acquired before out birth, has been lost in the sense that we are no longer directly aware of it and afterward by the use of the senses we recover that which we previously knew, this process that we speak of as learning is really a matter of recollection. The ideas that we recover in this way constitute the standard in comparison with which we judge the accuracy of that which is revealed through the senses. Thus, we are able to say of two objects that they are approximately equal, but insofar as their nature is revealed through the senses, they never reach perfect or absolute equality. In a similar manner, we may say that actions of a legal nature may approximate justice but absolute justice cannot be achieved, although it is an ideal toward which one may strive. The conclusion that may be drawn from these observations is that souls must have existed prior to the time when they entered human bodies. If absolute ideas existed before we were born, then our souls must have existed before we were born, for the ideas could not have existed apart from the souls that contained them.

Simmias then states that there is nothing that to his mind is more evident than the existence of such ideas as beauty, truth, justice, and the like. This, for him, is all the proof that is needed to establish the existence of souls prior to the birth of human beings. He believes that Cebes is also convinced that this is true, but there is one further question concerning which both Cebes and Simmias are in doubt. It has to do with the continued existence of souls after death. This is the other half of the argument, the proof of which is still wanting and needs to be supplied. Socrates contends that the proof has already been given, since it has been admitted that everything living has been born of the dead. If the soul existed before birth and in coming to life and being born can be born only from death and dying, it follows that it must continue to exist, since it has to be born again. He perceives, however, that Cebes and Simmias are not satisfied with this argument and he proceeds to probe deeper into the subject. Cebes thinks it is quite possible that souls, having entered human bodies and going out of them at the time of death, may be destroyed and come to an end.

In reply to Cebes' suggestion, Socrates calls attention to the fact that only compound or composite things are capable of being dissolved. That which is compounded, or made up of parts, is constantly changing, while that which is not compounded does not change but ever remains what it is. Things that are changing can be perceived by the senses but that which is unchanging cannot. Now the essences, or ideas of which we have been speaking such as justice, beauty, truth, and goodness, are simple and not compounded. They are unchanging and they cannot be perceived by the senses. Human nature contains two parts, which we call body and soul. The body is that part that is compounded, changing, and perceived by the senses. The soul in which the essences, or ideas, are present is uncompounded, changeless, and is not perceived by the senses. When the soul and the body are united, nature orders the soul to rule and govern and the body to obey and serve. In this respect the soul resembles the divine and the body that which is mortal. From this we may draw the conclusion that the "soul is in the very likeness of the divine, and immortal, and intelligible, and unchangeable; and the body is in the very likeness of the human, and mortal, and unintelligible, and multiform, and dissoluble, and changeable." When a man dies, the body, which is the visible part of man, becomes dissolved and decomposed but the same cannot be said of the soul. The truth is that the soul, which is pure at the time it departs from the body, contains no bodily taint and, being invisible, departs to the invisible world, which is divine and immortal and rational. There it continues to exist in bliss, being released from the error and folly of men, with their fears and wild passions and all other human ills, and dwells in the company of the gods.

While this might be true concerning the souls that were pure and uncontaminated by their contact with the body, what about those souls that had not remained pure? Was it not true that there are evil souls as well as good ones? What about the future of these evil souls when they are released from the body? Certainly, there would be no justice in treating both good and evil souls in the same way. Socrates recognizes the legitimacy of these questions and provides the best answer that he can, although he admits he has no positive proof concerning what will actually happen to the souls of men after they have been released from the bodies with which they have been associated. He is familiar with what the mystery cults of his day have to say on this matter, and he makes use of the myths that they have employed to indicate something like what he thinks would constitute an appropriate doctrine of rewards and punishments for good and evil souls, respectively.

The soul that has become polluted by being the companion and servant of the body, having become fascinated by the desires and pleasures of the body will, therefore, be impure at the time of departure. Souls of this nature, having become engrossed by the corporeal, will be compelled to wander about, prowling among tombs and sepulchers in payment of the penalty of their former evil way of life. They will continue to wander until the desires that haunt them have been satisfied, after which they will be imprisoned in another body. Those who have followed after gluttony, wantonness, and drunkenness will pass into asses and animals of that sort, while those who have chosen the part of injustice, tyranny, and violence will pass into wolves or hawks, or some other type of animal. All of them will be assigned to places corresponding to their several natures. Some of them, who have practiced the civil and social virtues by habit rather than reflection, may be expected to pass into some gentle social nature like that of bees or ants or even back again into some human form. Only those who are true lovers of wisdom and who are pure at the time of departing will be permitted to dwell with the gods.

After Socrates had finished speaking, all who were present remained silent for a few minutes, during which time they were given an opportunity to think about what they had been hearing. When asked about their opinion of the argument, Simmias replied that not all of his doubts have been removed. He mentions that both he and Cebes have certain questions that they would like to have clarified. Socrates is pleased to observe that they have open and inquiring minds and are ready to think for themselves rather than accept what they had been told them without subjecting it to the test of reasonableness. He informs them that if they will state their questions he will do his best to answer them. He is like the swan that sings its best song just prior to its final departure. His departure from this life is close at hand and his gift of prophecy should be at its best.

Simmias is disturbed with reference to the possibility of anyone having any objective knowledge about what happens to the soul after it has departed from the body. He believes it is quite proper for one to investigate the question so far as it is humanly possible, and he would consider anyone a coward who would refuse to look for proofs in support of what he believes to be true, but from what has been said so far concerning the future existence of the soul he finds that any positive proof is lacking. It seems to him that the argument Socrates has used about the soul could be applied with equal force to the harmony produced on a lyre. It could be said that harmony is a thing invisible, incorporeal, fair, divine, and abiding in the lyre that is harmonized but that the lyre and the strings are matter and composite, earthy, and akin to mortality. When someone breaks the lyre or cuts the strings what happens to the harmony? Even though it is of an invisible and heavenly nature, it will perish sooner than what remains of the broken lyre and its cut strings. It is conceivable that the body is a composite thing, the parts of which are strung or held together by the elements of hot and cold, wet and dry, and that the soul is the harmony, or due proportionate admixture, of them. If this is true would it not follow that when the strings of the body are unduly loosened or overstrained through disorder or other injury, the soul, although it is divine and immaterial, will like other harmonies of music or works of art perish at once, even before the material remains of the body have decayed or been burned?

Cebes disagrees with Simmias on one point, for he is convinced that the soul is stronger and more lasting than the body but he is in agreement with him that the continuous existence of the soul after death has not been proved. To make his position clear, he will compare the relationship between soul and body to that of a weaver and the coat he has been wearing. After the weaver dies, someone might argue that he still lives because the coat he has been accustomed to wear is still whole and undecayed, and since a man lasts longer than his coat, it must be that he is still alive. This, of course, would be nonsense, for everyone would know that a man may outwear several coats and the last one that he wears will still be in existence after he has died. But eventually even that coat will become old and decayed and cease to exist. May not the same thing be said of the soul? It was in existence prior to its entrance into a human body, and after it departs from that body, it will be born again in some other body. Just as the body of a man may outlast several coats, so the soul may outlast a number of bodies, but after a series of successive births, it seems quite possible that it may have become weary from these cycles of existence and at last succumb in one of the deaths and utterly perish.

Both Echecrates and Phaedo, after listening to these arguments, were seriously disturbed. It seemed to them that, while Socrates had presented good arguments in support of his position, Cebes and Simmias had been successful in refuting them. They were beginning to wonder whether

anything was to be gained by argumentation, since apparently it was leading to no definite conclusion. At this point Socrates warns against the
dangers of becoming misologists, who have no faith in the reasoning process. He explains that it is not reasoning that is at fault but rather the
failure of men to reason correctly. He then proceeds to answer each of the
arguments presented by Cebes and Simmias. He begins by asking Simmias
if he is still in agreement with the doctrine that knowledge is recollection
and that from this it can be inferred that souls have existed prior to their
entrance into bodies. When Simmias replies in the affirmative, he is reminded of the fact that this is not in agreement with the idea that the soul is a
harmony that is made out of strings set in the frame of the body. The reason
for this is that harmony cannot exist prior to the elements out of which it is
composed. The truth is that harmony is not a sort of thing like the soul. The
lyre and the strings must exist first and then harmony is made last of all, although it perishes first. Then, too, it must be recognized that there are different degrees of harmony but this is not true of the soul. These considerations
are sufficient to refute the idea that the soul is comparable to the harmony
that ceases to exist when the lyre is broken or its strings have been cut.

Socrates' reply to Cebes is somewhat longer, since it involves the whole
question of generation and corruption. Although Cebes admits that the
soul is superior to the body, he maintains it is impossible to know whether
the soul, having worn out many bodies, may not perish itself, leaving its last
body behind, and this would mean death not only of the body but of the soul,
for in the body the work of destruction never ceases. In order to convince
Cebes that the soul is really immortal and will never perish, Socrates reports some of the changes that have taken place in his own thinking with
reference to this problem. When he was young he became interested in the
natural sciences, for he believed they could help him to understand the
causes of things and to know why they were created or destroyed. He made
inquiries about the growth and decay of animals as well as the origin of
thought. He soon began to doubt that growth is merely the result of eating
and drinking or that the brain is the cause of thought. He came to the conclusion that the physical sciences could provide no answers to the questions he had in mind. A common error consisted in the failure to distinguish
between the condition of a thing and its cause. To regard material things as
the cause of thought would imply that Socrates is sitting where he is because he is made up of bones and muscles rather than giving the true reason,
which is that he is sitting here because the Athenians thought it good to
sentence him to death. In connection with the idea that opposites generate
opposites, Socrates explains that this has been affirmed not of opposite ideas
either in us or in nature, but of opposite things—not of life and death, but
of individuals living and dying. Not only does life exclude death but the
soul, of which life is the inseparable attribute, also excludes death and this
means that the soul is immortal.

If the soul is immortal what manner of person ought we to be? This question must be answered, not merely with reference to time but to eternity as well. Death is not the end of all and the wicked is not released from his evil by death, for after death the soul is carried away to judgment. After receiving punishment, it returns to earth in the course of ages. The wise soul is guided through the windings of the world below, but the impure soul wanders hither and thither without a guide and is carried at last to its own place.

After Socrates had finished speaking, Crito asked if he had any requests to make concerning his children or any other matters. Socrates replied that his only wish was that they look after themselves properly and live in accordance with the principles that he has taught. That would be the greatest service that they could perform for him. When asked in what way he would like to be buried, Socrates replied "In any way that you like; only you must get hold of me, and take care that I do not walk away from you." He then explained that he cannot make Crito believe that he is the same Socrates who has been talking. Crito fancies that he is the other Socrates, whom he will soon see as a dead body, and that is why he asks how he shall be buried. Socrates then adds these words, "Be of good cheer, then, my dear Crito, and say that you are burying my body only, and do with that as is usual, and as you think best."

When he had spoken these words, Socrates arose and went to the bath chamber with Crito. After he had finished his bath, his children and the women of his family were brought to him. He talked to them and gave them a few instructions in the presence of Crito, after which he dismissed them and returned to the members of the group. The jailer soon appeared and administered the poison. When it had begun to take effect he uncovered his face and said "Crito, I owe a cock to Asclepius; will you remember to pay the debt?" Crito answered that it would be paid. In a few moments the attendants uncovered him and found that his eyes were set. Crito then closed his eyes and mouth. Phaedo then remarks "Such was the end, Echecrates, of our friend, whom I may truly call the wisest, and justest, and best of all men whom I have ever known."

Commentary

The *Phaedo* is one of Plato's dialogs in which the dramatic form of art achieved its highest level of development. It consists of a series of conversations supposed to have taken place before a numerous audience. The purpose of these conversations was to reveal what had actually taken place in the prison on the last day that Socrates was alive. Phaedo, who for a long time had been a close and intimate friend of Socrates, was one of those who were present on that occasion, and he relates what had taken place, including the rather lengthy conversations as he remembers them. The place where this narration occurred is Phlius, a town of Sicyon, where Phaedo of Elis had stopped on his way home from Athens. The story is told to a group of Phliasian admirers of Socrates who had not yet learned of the details connected with his imprisonment and death. Echecrates, who was a member of the group, was a Pythagorean and two other members of the group, Cebes and Simmias, were pupils of the Pythagorean teacher Philolaus. From these facts it seems likely that the gathering took place in the meetinghouse of the local Pythagoreans.

We do not know the exact order in which Plato's dialogs were written, but it seems fairly certain that the *Phaedo* was not one of the early Socratic dialogs written during his more youthful period nor was it a product of his late or more advanced years. Apparently, it belongs to the middle period of his literary career, when his maturity as a writer had reached its highest stage. Evidently, Plato intended his readers to regard this dialog as an accurate record of the way in which Socrates spent his last hours on earth. It would be of particular interest to note the topics on which he spoke with his intimate friends in the face of his imminent death. The authenticity of the record is indicated by the fact that a list is given of the names of the people who were present. Since the most of these people were probably still living when the *Phaedo* was published, any errors in the account would have been noted and brought to light. Although Plato was not one of those present at the meeting, he was in all likelihood well informed concerning what had taken place. We know that after the death of Socrates he spent some time at Megara, where he had ample opportunity to meet and talk with some of the persons mentioned in the dialog. Phaedo, who was the narrator, is represented in the dialog as a mere lad and it is quite reasonable to imagine he was well acquainted with Plato during his later years.

Taken as a whole, the subject matter of the dialog is Socrates' conception of the soul. Its purpose was to state as clearly as possible his reasons for believing that the soul is not only immortal in the sense that it has no beginning and no end but that it partakes of the very nature of divinity. Hence, an imitation of God becomes a right and reasonable standard of conduct for human beings. The argument of the dialog is moral, insofar as it maintains that the dignity and worth of the soul affords sufficient grounds for believing that death to a good man means entrance into a better life that is something that he may face with good comfort. The dialog contains a whole series of arguments in support of belief in the immortality of the soul. No one of these should be regarded as sufficient by itself to establish complete proof of immortality. Rather, the evidence is cumulative and taken together it constitutes a strong case for acceptance of the belief. At any rate, Socrates is able to make an adequate reply to opponents of the belief in immortality, including those who have advocated epiphenomenalism and a mechanical conception of nature.

The reader of the dialog is bound to be impressed by the courage and fortitude that Socrates possesses in the face of imminent death. Nevertheless, he has often been criticized for his role as a husband and a father. The fact that his wife, Xanthippe, and their infant son were excluded from the company of visitors who had arrived at the prison on the last day of his life has sometimes been regarded as evidence of harshness in his attitude toward them. This is not necessarily the case. They are conducted home at the beginning of the discourse because Xanthippe is said to have been on the verge of a nervous breakdown, and Socrates wishes to spare both her and himself. It is also important to note that the children and the "ladies of the family" appear again toward the close of the dialog. The wife and infant son are believed to have spent the last night of his life with him. He has a final interview with the members of the family and we are told that the interview was a lengthy one. The interview is not described because Phaedo did not witness it. Except for Crito, the oldest friend of the family, the interview was a private family affair.

When Socrates remarks that a true philosopher is one who is willing and ready to die but believes it would be wrong for anyone to put an end to his own life, Cebes wants to know why it would be wrong for one to commit suicide. Knowing that Cebes was a Pythagorean, Socrates asked if his teacher Philolaus had not explained to him the reasons for condemning actions of that type. Cebes replied that the explanations had been given but he was never able to understand them. He was now hoping that Socrates would make it clear to him. In common with some of the mystery cults, especially the Orphic mysteries, the Pythagoreans had accepted the idea that the hardships of human life are punishments for evil deeds that were committed in some former existence. Socrates does not indicate that he is in full accord with what has been taught about one's prenatal existence, but he does find an answer to Cebes' question about suicide in the Pythagorean doctrine that human beings are chattels, or possessions, in the hands of the gods. For this reason they are not at liberty to destroy that which is not their own but belongs to beings other than themselves.

Granting that it is wrong for one to put an end to his own life unless commanded to do so by the gods, Socrates then goes on to explain why it is that a true philosopher, or lover of wisdom, has no fear of death. He points out that the faith and hope with which the philosopher faces death is in perfect harmony with the principles by which he has regulated his whole life. The world may not be aware of it, but the fact is that the whole life of philosophy is but one long rehearsal of dying. Because the world does not understand the meaning of dying, they accuse philosophers of being morbid but in this they are mistaken, for death is nothing other than the release of the soul from the body. It is the achievement of the soul's independence and this is what the philosopher has been trying to accomplish throughout his entire life. Placing only a lesser value on the gratification of physical appetites and the acquisition of material goods, he is concerned primarily with the development of the soul. In his pursuit of knowledge, he finds the demands of the body to be a real hindrance and he tries as best he can to escape them. That is why he puts his trust in thinking rather than in what is experienced through the senses, for in thinking the soul is independent of the body in a way that is not true of the senses. Bodily wants and passions are the chief causes of war and competition in business, two occupations of the so-called active life that leave little time for thinking and the pursuit of knowledge. This is why the person who is in love with knowledge knows that his heart's desire will be achieved either after death or not at all.

Now that the philosopher's attitude toward death has been explained satisfactorily, Simmias remarks that the existence of the soul after death appears to have been assumed without any evidence or proof to support such a belief. He mentions that many persons believe the soul is dispersed like smoke at the time of death and he sees no reason why this belief should be rejected. If Socrates can convince him that the soul does continue to exist after death, he would like for him to present the evidence on which his opinion is based. It is important to note that Simmias is not asking for complete proof and Socrates is not promising to do anything more than show that immortality of the soul is more likely to be true than a denial of it. The argument consists of two parts, each of which is designed to support belief in the continued existence of the soul following the death of the body. The first part makes reference to the ancient belief in the doctrine of rebirth. It was a part of the teachings of the Orphic mystery cult, according to which a soul that is born into this world has come back from another world and will eventually return to it. While there is no indication that Socrates accepted everything taught by these mystery cults, the very fact that belief in the rebirth of the soul has been held by so many persons over a long period of time lends some support to the idea. A stronger reason for believing in the survival of the soul can be found in the doctrine of opposites and the way in which they are related to one another. According to this view, the world is made up of pairs of opposites such as hot and cold, great and small, good and bad, etc. Furthermore, it can be said universally that whatever comes to be does so out of its opposite. Day comes out of night and night comes out of day. That which becomes less must have once been greater and then become less. The weaker is generated from the stronger and the swifter from the slower. Now, the opposite of life is death, and since opposites are generated out of one another, we may conclude that life is generated out of death and death is generated out of life. If all things that partake of life were to die and after they are dead remain in that form and not come to life again, eventually there would be nothing alive on the earth. From this we may conclude that death is not the final end of one's existence but only a transition.

The general conception of the world as made up of "pairs of opposites" that change from one to the other was a Greek notion that had been held for a long time. It was especially prominent in the teachings of Heraclitus, who had coordinated sleeping with waking and life with death. It was also a part of the Pythagorean philosophy, with which Cebes, Simmias, and other members of the group were familiar. It was not, however, a cogent piece of reasoning, since it ignores the distinction between condition and cause, a point that Socrates apparently recognized at a later stage in the discussion. It is true that day follows night just as night follows day, but this does not mean that either one is made "out of" the other or that one is changed into the other. Cold is the opposite of heat but it is not true that either one is changed into or actually becomes the other. Nevertheless, the doctrine concerning opposites was useful for the purpose that Socrates had in mind, since it was based on assumptions that were regarded as true by members of the group to whom he was speaking. The effectiveness of the argument is strengthened when it is combined with the second part, which has to do with the doctrine of reminiscence.

According to this doctrine, what we usually refer to as learning the truth is really a matter of remembering something that has been forgotten. That which the soul possessed in a former existence can be brought to mind through the use of a proper stimulus. In some instances, this can be accomplished simply by asking a number of questions. For example, in the dialog called *Meno* Socrates asks an uneducated slave about the proof of a certain theorem in geometry. At first the slave appears to be entirely ignorant of the proof but after he has been asked a number of questions he sees it as clearly as anyone. Socrates then remarks that the slave now knows the proof and yet he has not told him anything. He has merely asked him some questions. Obviously, the slave has possessed this knowledge all the time but has been unable to recall it until appropriate questions had been put to him.

The strongest evidence in support of the reminiscence theory, or doctrine of recollection, comes from an examination of the way in which knowledge of universals is obtained. Ideas such as justice, beauty, truth, goodness, equality, and others are acknowledged to be real and it is possible for individuals to know what they mean. At the same time, it must be admitted that none of these ideas have ever been perceived by the senses nor have they been experienced in their pure form. Objects may appear to be equal and actions may approximate the ideal of justice, but no two objects can ever be said to be exactly equal nor is perfect justice ever achieved in human experience. How then is it possible for anyone to know what justice is or what equality really means? The answer, according to this theory, is that the ideas are remembered from a former existence. Sense experiences serve as a stimulus to the mind, causing it to remember or recollect that which is already present within it. Without this awareness of the meaning of universals, the whole process of knowing would be impossible. For instance, when anyone is asked what a particular object is the answer, if one is to be given at all, will consist of saying that it belongs to a certain class of objects and these class names are necessarily examples of universals, or ideas, in their pure form. From this analysis of the knowing process, it follows that souls must have existed prior to one's birth, for otherwise the ideas could not have been carried from one existence to another. The souls in which these ideas were present were not only in existence but they were actively intelligent.

Cebes and Simmias both express their satisfaction with the proof offered in support of the belief that souls exist prior to the birth of human beings, but neither of them is fully convinced that souls will continue their existence after death. Simmias suggests the possibility that souls are like the smoke that comes out of a chimney and then disintegrates into thin air and vanishes away. Socrates then reminds him that it is only composite things that are capable of disintegration. Objects of this nature can be perceived by the senses and they are always subject to change. Objects that are not compounded but are simple in their nature always remain what they are. They are not subject to change and neither can they be perceived by the senses. This is what has been admitted concerning universals, or the abstract ideas that are present in souls. It is, therefore, reasonable to conclude that souls, like the ideas that are present in them, are not subject to change. They are simple rather than compound in nature, and for this reason they cannot disintegrate or cease to exist.

Two of the chief arguments against belief in the immortality of the soul are brought into the discussion and Socrates has a reply to each of them. The one that is often referred to as epiphenomenalism is introduced by Simmias and the other one, which involves a mechanistic conception of life and the world, is presented by Cebes. Epiphenomenalism is the doctrine that souls or spiritual substances are the product of matter and with the destruction of the matter that produced them they will cease to exist. Simmias compares the soul to the harmony that is produced by a lyre in the hands of a musician. The harmony has many of the same characteristics that have been ascribed to the soul. It is immaterial and partakes of a divine quality. What happens to the harmony when the lyre is broken or its strings are cut? Obviously, the harmony will cease to exist. It is dependent on the material instrument from which it is produced and will perish with the destruction of that instrument. May not the same thing be true of the soul? So long as the soul is united with the body it is dependent upon it. The body, being composed of material substances, will in time disintegrate and cease to exist and this might very well mean that the soul, like the harmony of the lyre, will perish along with it.

Socrates' reply to Simmias takes into account some of the more important differences between the soul and the harmony produced by a musical instrument. The relationship of the soul to the body is in one respect quite different from that of harmony to the material instrument on which it is dependent. It is the function of the soul to rule or govern the body rather than to be served by it. Therefore, the soul is not dependent on the body in the same way that harmony is dependent on the lyre. The soul is in one sense the permanent and divine element in a human being, while the body is a mortal and changing element. Hence, we should expect the body to be perishable and the soul to be imperishable. Particular emphasis is given to the deification, or divine character, of the soul in contrast to the human and mortal nature of the body. While it is true that the soul, when united with the body, may be influenced by the passions and desires of the body and in this respect we may speak of the souls that are evil, it is also true that in its real nature the soul is constantly trying to be free of the demands of the body. This process of becoming free of the body is the means by which it achieves deification and that which is divine can never perish.

A mechanistic conception of life and the world apparently forms the basis for Cebes' final objection to belief in the immortality of the soul. Using the figure of a weaver who wears out a number of coats, he asks if it may not be true that the soul, having gone through a number of rebirths, will at last succumb in one of its deaths and utterly perish? In a rather lengthy reply to Cebes, Socrates reviews some of his own experiences in trying to find the meaning of life through a study of the physical sciences. As a result of his many investigations, he had become convinced that it is impossible to learn anything about the spiritual life of man from a study of the material aspects of his nature. The physical sciences are useful as a means of recording the order in which movements observed by the senses take place, but they tell us nothing about the purpose or meaning of life nor do they reveal what is right or wrong in the moral sense in which those terms are used. He concludes his remarks on this subject by referring again to the so-called doctrine of opposites and pointing out that pairs of opposites such as "hot and cold," "day and night," "life and death," and similar ones are not changed one into the other. While it is true that one of the opposites in each pair is followed by the other, this does not mean that one of them is the cause of the other or that the nature of any one of the opposites has been changed in the least. To imagine that one of them has been changed into the other is the result of a failure to distinguish between condition and cause. The nature of being hot is never changed into the nature of being cold, day is never changed into night, and the nature of life is never changed into the nature of death. Each of these opposites always remains exactly what it is, and from this we can infer that the soul that is present in the human body will not change its nature by passing from a state of existence into one of nonexistence.

With regard to the distinction between good souls and evil ones, Socrates recognizes that freedom of choice is given to each individual. The soul that yields to the appetites and desires of the body by placing a higher value on sensual pleasures and material possessions than it does on wisdom and righteous conduct is an evil one, while souls that resist temptations of this kind and strive toward perfection of both mind and conduct are designated as good ones. Because he believes in the justice of God he is confident that a different fate is in store for good and evil souls. Just how this will be accomplished he is not certain, but the doctrine of reincarnation as set forth in the teachings of the mystery religions offers a solution that he believes is at least something like what will take place. Evil souls will be reincarnated in the bodies of different kinds of animals and insects and always with the possibility of entering into higher forms of life. The good souls will be treated in a manner that is proportionate to their degrees of goodness, with the final goal of dwelling eternally with the gods.

The events that are related toward the end of the dialog are of particular significance in revealing somewhat further the true character of Socrates. His concern for the welfare of his wife and children, his request that a small debt that he owed be paid, his kindly attitude toward the attendant who administers the poison, his faith in what lies beyond death, and above all the courage and nobility with which he accepts his fate, are all indications of his goodness. Of him it has well been said that he acquired the art of dying beautifully. Phaedo's final tribute to him is apparently well deserved.

REVIEW QUESTIONS AND ESSAY TOPICS

1. What are our chief sources of information concerning the life and teachings of Socrates? Why did he leave no writings?
2. Describe briefly the dialectic method as it was used by Socrates. Explain what is meant by the statement "virtue is knowledge."
3. In what respect was Socrates opposed to a democratic system of government? Explain his lack of interest in the physical sciences.
4. Give a brief account of the life and times of Plato, including his education, travels, and writings.
5. In what respect was Plato in favor of democracy and in what respect was he opposed to it? What did Plato regard as the ideal form of government?
6. Describe Plato's experiments in government at Syracuse. Why did these experiments fail? How was Plato rescued?
7. Name some of the most important of Plato's dialogs and indicate the chief subject matter of each of them.

8. Describe the nature of the Academy that was founded by Plato. What were the chief advantages of the dialog form of writing?

9. Who was Euthyphro? What is the chief subject matter of the dialog that bears his name?

10. What were the circumstances that led Euthyphro to charge his own father with the crime of murder?

11. Contrast the two conceptions relative to the purpose of religion held by Euthyphro and Socrates.

12. Describe Euthyphro's attempts to define piety and tell why Socrates objected to each of them.

13. Why do you think the dialog *Euthyphro* closed without reaching any satisfactory definition of piety? What purpose was the dialog intended to accomplish? Do you think it succeeded?

14. The *Apology* is believed to contain an authentic account of Socrates' defense of himself. What are the reasons for this?

15. Socrates states that he will reply to two kinds of accusation brought against him. What were they and why did he find it so difficult to deal with the first one?

16. How did Socrates reconcile the statement made by the oracle at Delphi that he was the wisest man in Athens with his own profession of ignorance?

17. How did Socrates account for the popular prejudice that led so many people to be suspicious of him and his work?

18. What, according to Meletus, was the crime of which Socrates was accused? What do you think was the real reason why Meletus was opposed to Socrates?

19. How did Socrates reply to the charge that he was a corrupter of the youth? What was it that led people to think he was guilty?

20. Aristophanes in his work called *The Clouds* had made certain references to Socrates. For what purpose had these remarks been made and how were they interpreted by Socrates' opponents?

21. Socrates did not charge fees for his services as a teacher. Since he did not think it was wrong to charge fees and since he was in need of money, why did he not accept fees?

22. Why did Socrates reject many of the popular beliefs concerning the Athenian gods? Was Socrates an atheist? Give reasons for your answer.

23. What reason did Socrates give for having avoided a political career? Describe the prophetic warning that he delivered to the judges at the close of his address.

24. Why was Socrates kept in prison for a whole month preceding his execution? What reasons were given by Crito for urging him to escape?

25. Why did Socrates believe it would be wrong for him to escape? Did he believe all laws authorized by the state should be obeyed?
26. How did Socrates reconcile his position about obedience to the laws of the state with his conviction that it is morally right to disobey laws that are unjust? Distinguish moral and legal rights.
27. What is the chief subject matter of the *Phaedo*? Since it was written months or possibly years after the death of Socrates, what reasons can be given for its authenticity as a correct account?
28. Explain Socrates' statement that the life of philosophy is a "longing for death." Was this consistent with his refusal to escape from prison?
29. What was the Heraclitean doctrine concerning "opposites"? What use did Socrates make of it in his reply to Cebes and Simmias?
30. How did Socrates refute the idea advanced by Simmias that the soul is comparable to the harmony of a musical instrument?
31. What arguments did Socrates use in his refutation of both epiphenomenalism and a mechanistic interpretation of the soul?
32. Explain Socrates' theory of "recollection" and its bearing on belief in the immortality of the soul.
33. It has often been held that Socrates was delinquent in his role as a husband and a father. What reasons can be given both for and against this belief?
34. Tell why you think Phaedo's final tribute to Socrates was or was not well deserved.

SELECTED BIBLIOGRAPHY

Ballard, G. *Socratic Ignorance*. The Hague: Nijhoff Press, 1965. Examples of Socratic irony are given with explanations of the way in which these were used to refute the claims of the Sophists.

Cornford, Francis M. *Before and after Socrates*. Cambridge: Cambridge University Press, 1968. The life and teachings of Socrates are presented in relation to the Sophistic movement that preceded him and also his relation to later schools of philosophy.

Cross, Robert Nicol. *Socrates, the Man and His Mission*. Freeport, N.Y.: Books for Libraries Press, 1970. An account of the life of Socrates, with particular emphasis on the way in which he conceived his work as a response to a divine command.

Eliot, Alexander. *Socrates, the Person and the Portrait*. New York: Crown Publishers, 1967. A relatively short account of the life and teachings of Socrates, showing how he appeared to his contemporaries and to suceeding generations.

Field, G. C. *Plato and His Contemporaries.* New York: Dutton, 1930. A full account of the life and teachings of Plato, including his relationship to Socrates and to the Heraclitean and Eleatic schools of philosophy.

Plato. *The Death of Socrates,* trans. Romano Guardini. Cleveland: World, 1962. The story of the trial and death of Socrates as related in four of the Platonic dialogs that have to do with that theme.

_____. *Dialogues,* trans. Benjamin Jowett. 4th ed. Oxford: Clarendon Press, 1953. A great classic. One of the oldest (1871) and most widely used of the translations into English. An extensive introduction is included with each of the dialogs.

_____. *The Last Days of Socrates,* trans. Hugh Tredennick. Baltimore: Penguin, 1954. Includes the *Apology, Crito,* and *Phaedo,* with an introduction and notes.

_____. *The Trial and Death of Socrates,* trans. John Warrington. New York: Dutton, 1963. A translation of four dialogs dealing with this subject, accompanied by an introduction to each of them.

Rogers, Arthur Kenyon. *The Socratic Problem.* New Haven, Conn.: Yale University Press, 1933. A comparison and an evaluation of three different conceptions of Socrates based on passages found in the various dialogs.

Taylor, Alfred Edward. *Plato, the Man and His Works.* New York: Meridian Books, 1960. One of the best and most widely used commentaries on Plato's dialogs. An extensive account, along with a critical evaluation of each of the more important dialogs.

_____. *Socrates.* Garden City, N.Y.: Doubleday, 1954. A full account of the life and teachings of Socrates by one of the best known historians of early Greek philosophy.

NOTES

Your Guides to Successful Test Preparation.

Cliffs Test Preparation Guides

Efficient preparation means better test scores. Go with the experts and use **Cliffs Test Preparation Guides.** They'll help you reach your goals because they're: Complete • Concise • Functional • In-depth. They are focused on helping you know what to expect from each test. The test-taking techniques have been proven in classroom programs nationwide.

Recommended for individual use or as a part of formal test preparation programs.